GRACE AND THE GENTILES

GRACE AND THE GENTILES

*Expository Studies in
six Pauline Letters*

by
Marcus L. Loane

THE BANNER OF TRUTH TRUST

THE BANNER OF TRUTH TRUST
3 Murrayfield Road, Edinburgh EH12 6EL
P O Box 621, Carlisle, Pennsylvania 17013, USA

*

© Marcus L. Loane 1981
First published 1981
ISBN 0 85151 327 1

*

Filmset, printed and bound in Great Britain by
Hazell Watson & Viney Ltd, Aylesbury, Bucks

This book is for
Peter and Vandhy
whom God has called
out of darkness into His marvellous light

FOREWORD

WHEN THE aged Simeon held the Christ-Child in his arms and prayed that he might depart in peace, it was on the ground that he had seen the One whom God had appointed for our salvation: 'A light to lighten the Gentiles, and the glory of thy people Israel' (Luke 2:32 A.V.). That Child was set for the fall and rising again of many in Israel, but His life did not touch many who were Gentiles. There was the Roman centurion of whom He said: 'I have not found so great faith, no, not in Israel' (Matt. 8:10). There was the Syro-Phoenician woman of whom He said: 'O woman, great is thy faith: be it unto thee even as thou wilt' (Matt. 15:28). There were the Greeks who came to Philip with their earnest request: 'Sir, we would see Jesus' (John 12:21). Jesus Himself declared that the time will come when 'they shall come from the east and west, and from the north and south, and shall sit down in the kingdom of God' (Luke 13:29). But that vision belonged to the future. Among His last words to the Twelve was the command that they should bear witness to Him from the Jews in Jerusalem to the Gentiles in the ends of the earth (Acts 1:8). It was Simon Peter who first proclaimed the Name of Christ to the Gentile Cornelius, and it was the anonymous evangelists of Antioch who first began to preach to the Gentiles without regard to the claims of Judaism. But the pre-eminent evangelist of the Gentiles was Paul. His whole life was dedicated to this mission from the time when he heard the call of God: 'I will send thee forth far hence unto the Gentiles' (Acts 22:21). He was thenceforth unfaltering in his dedication to the cause of Christ among the Gentiles, in spite of the opposition, contradiction, and persecution that came upon him. And his Letters show that apart from the glory of Christ Himself, the cause of the Gentiles was that which lay nearest his heart.

It is common to think of the Pauline Letters as if they were easily divisible into four groups. The first group consists of the two Epistles to the Thessalonians. These must have been written during his long sojourn in Corinth as part of the second missionary journey; it is almost certain that they are the earliest epistles to have survived. The next group may be called the four Great Epistles, namely, 1 and 2 Corinthians written in Ephesus, Galatians and Romans written in Corinth, in the course of the third missionary journey. The third group is known as the four Prison Epistles. It consists of Philippians which stands apart from the others, and of Ephesians, Colossians and Philemon which are closely related. These three seem to have been written while he was in prison in Rome; they belong together for a variety of reasons. The Epistle to Philippi may have been written towards the end of that imprisonment when his trial was nearing its crisis and climax. But it contains such clear echoes of the thought and language of Galatians and Romans that it may belong to an earlier period and an imprisonment perhaps in Ephesus. The fourth group is that of the three Pastoral Epistles, 1 and 2 Timothy and Titus. These were written during the last phase of his life; 2 Timothy in particular was written during his final imprisonment and not long before his martyrdom. This corpus of thirteen Letters does not represent all the correspondence for which Paul was responsible. There is clear evidence for example that there were at least two other Letters to the Church at Corinth which have not survived. But these thirteen Letters are invaluable: they not only furnish the strong foundation for the doctrines of grace, but they also afford unique insight into the needs of the churches in the first Christian century.

This book is a series of studies in six of the thirteen Letters; namely all those in the first and third groups. I have chosen a key verse or passage from each chapter in each Letter and have tried to expound it with reverence and with clarity. There can be no greater fascination in the study of Paul's writings than to see through the text into his mind, to trace his thought process, and to perceive what led him to formulate argument or to express himself in the way that he did. I have used the text of the Revised Version (1881) throughout unless another translation has been indicated. I am grateful to Word Books for generous permission to reprint material from my earlier book, *Three Letters From Prison*, published in 1972. The chapters on Ephesians Six, Colossians Four, and The Epistle to Philemon, are taken from that book with only minor variations.

One may learn what manner of man Paul was from his self-revealing letters. There have been few men in Christian history whose lives were so crowded with travel, service, evangelism and activity or with hardship, ordeal, privation and suffering. His personality throbs with intense feeling; his faith was indomitable; and his passion for Christ was unquenchable. But what was he like in personal appearance? There is little to tell, but he himself implied that it was neither attractive nor impressive. There was little that would command respect on sight. He was weak and of no account in his bodily presence; he was rude or contemptible in speech (cf. 2 Cor. 10:1,10; 11:6). He bore branded in his body the scars of the stones at Lystra (Gal. 6:17). Various traditions were in vogue in early literature. Nicephorus Callistus has left the most circumstantial account.[1] 'St. Paul', he wrote, 'was small of stature, stooping, and rather inclinable to crookedness, pale-faced, of an elderly look, bald on the head; his eyes lively, keen, and cheerful, shaded in part by his eyebrows which hung a little over; his nose, rather long and ungracefully bent; his beard, pretty thick of hair, and of a sufficient length; and like his locks, interspersed with grey'. Nevertheless in spite of weak eyes (cf. Gal. 4:15), and a poor presence, and a thorn in the flesh, he could say with simple finality: 'By the grace of God, I am what I am' (1 Cor. 15:10). His duty and delight were to preach Jesus as the Lord, and if he named himself at all, it was only as the bondslave of his Gentile converts for Jesus' sake. This is the man whose voice we hear in word and phrase, after the lapse of centuries and through the medium of an English translation, striving above all to commend the Lord, even Jesus, the Christ, to the end of time and to the ends of the earth.

[1]. *Lib.* ii, cap. 37

Chapter One

Not In Word Only

'Our Gospel came not unto you in word only, but also in power, and in the Holy Ghost, and in much assurance.'

1 THESSALONIANS 1:1-5

THESSALONICA WAS the flourishing capital of the Province of Macedonia in the northern half of modern Greece. It had the great natural advantage of a splendid harbour, situated in the middle of the bend of the Thermaic gulf; Xerxes indeed chose it as his naval base for his march on Greece, and it helped to make the city a great maritime and commercial centre. Thessalonica was in fact the key to the whole Province, because it also occupied a strategic site on the Via Egnatia, the great highroad which linked Rome with the East. Here Paul came with Silas and Timothy sometime between 50 and 52 A.D. They had travelled on foot from the Roman colony of Philippi about one hundred miles to the east, spending three days on the journey. They came in the hey-day of its fame and prosperity when its citizens could be described by Cicero as 'lying in the lap' of the Roman Empire.[1] Paul was able to preach in the synagogue for three successive sabbaths, 'opening and alleging that it behoved the Christ to suffer and to rise again from the dead, and that this Jesus, whom, said he, I proclaim unto you, is the Christ' (Acts 17:3). He was driven out in the end, and turned at once to the Gentiles. This infuriated the Jews who set out to provoke the city rabble to create an uproar. The mob failed to track Paul down, but seized Jason and some others, and dragged them before the magistrates or politarchs with the accusation: 'These that have turned the

[1] Cicero, de prov. consul, 2.cf. J. B. Lightfoot: *Biblical Essays*, p. 255.

I

world upside down are come hither also . . . and . . . act contrary
to the decrees of Caesar, saying that there is another king, one
Jesus' (Acts 17:6-7). As a result, Paul and his companions were
compelled to leave the city, first for Beroea, then for Athens; but
he sent Timothy back to Thessalonica and left Silas in Beroea to
strengthen his converts. They rejoined him at length in Corinth,
and brought news that gladdened his heart.

Perhaps it was early in A.D. 51 or 52 that his Epistle was
written, the first Pauline letter to have survived, and it begins
with a salutation which was stamped with dignity as well as with
brevity: 'Paul, and Silvanus, and Timothy, unto the church of
the Thessalonians in God the Father and the Lord Jesus Christ:
Grace to you and peace' (1:1). This is the shortest of all his
introductions, but it contains all the essential elements; namely,
the address to the church, linking it with the Father and the Son,
and greetings of grace and peace. The phrase *in* God the Father
and the Lord Jesus Christ' is only found once, apart from this
verse (2 Thess. 1:1), and it is all the more remarkable because it
was employed within twenty years of Christ's death and resurrection. Elsewhere Paul wrote to 'all that are in Rome', or to 'the
church of God which is at Corinth', and so on (Rom. 1:7, 1 Cor.
1:2, etc.). But he addressed himself in this Letter to 'the Church
of the Thessalonians in God'. Nor is that all; the reference is
amplified with an unselfconscious ease as he linked 'the Father
and the Lord Jesus Christ'. He wanted those converts to take in
the reality of their union with God; they were *in* Him, and that
gave them perfect security in a world of hostile persecution.
Therefore he gave them his customary greeting: 'Grace to you,
and peace'. *Grace* was the Greek salutation; *peace* was the Hebrew
greeting. These two words combine all that is joyous, tender,
loving, gracious. The same two words stand at the head of all his
Letters with only one variation: the Epistles to Timothy add one
more word: 'grace, mercy, peace' (1 Tim. 1:2; 2 Tim. 1:2). There
is a sense in which those words sum up the whole message of the
Gospel, whether for Jew or for Gentile.

Paul went on at once to pour out his heart in the spirit of
thankful and comprehensive recollection: 'We give thanks to

God always for you all, making mention of you in our prayers, remembering without ceasing your work of faith and labour of love and patience of hope in our Lord Jesus Christ, before our God and Father' (1:2-3). Memory and thanksgiving were stimulants to prayer, and what he had in mind was that triad of virtues which were so often linked in his thinking. Thus he had in continual remembrance their *work of faith*. Elsewhere the two concepts of faith and works are set in sharp contrast; but here they are boldly combined. Another translation makes the point clear: 'your work produced by faith' (N.I.V.) The same point is brought out elsewhere: 'faith working through love' (Gal. 5:6). But what is meant by faith? Fides est fiducia: so said the great masters of the Reformation. No one can too distinctly recollect that *faith* means *trust*, and the supreme object of trust is the Person of Christ Himself. Faith gives us our first sight of One whom our eyes can not as yet see, but whom we love and in whom we ever rejoice. Faith is like the hand that opens the door so that the Lord Christ may come and dwell within. Such faith draws all its strength and vitality from Him, for it receives Him and unites the soul with Him in a union that not even death can dissolve. It is not a thing of virtue; it has nothing to do with merit; it can not be generated by our own self-effort; it is the gift of God; and this faith must come first, both in theology and in experience. So it was in the case of John Wesley on May 24th 1738 at the little Moravian meeting in London's Aldersgate Street. 'I felt my heart strangely warmed', he wrote; 'I felt I did *trust in Christ*, Christ alone, for salvation'.[2]

Then he remembered without ceasing their *labour of love*; that is, 'labour prompted by love' (N.I.V.). Faith does not lead to a selfish spirit or an exclusive piety; its first glorious consequence is love for Christ and for all His people. Paul chose the word that spoke of love in its distinctive Christian meaning, and such love should always be a growing reality in our experience. 'And this I pray', he wrote to his Philippian converts, 'that your love may abound yet more and more' (Phil. 1:9). It ought to flow like a river in flood; it should break all its banks. Love is often far too shallow, and if not that, then it is too narrow; it needs both depth

[2] cf. John Telford: *The Life of John Wesley* p. 101 (my italics).

and breadth. Then it will bring better knowledge of God, and better understanding of others. So the heart in which the Lord Christ dwells will expand with 'the love . . . which passeth knowledge' (Eph. 3:19). That love will be centred on Christ Himself, but its circumference will take in 'all the saints' without regard to class, race or culture (cf. Eph. 1:15; Col. 1:4). This is rooted in one of the final sayings of the Lord Jesus: 'A new commandment I give unto you, that ye love one another' (John 13:34). It was not like that in Jewish circles; nor was it like that in Gentile quarters. But as He had loved them, so they were to love one another; and as disciples multiplied, they were called to fashion their lives in the very spirit of this saying. This was indeed something new in human society; it was the warm comprehensive love that finds a willing outlet in service for others. The Lord Jesus placed it on the highest level when He went on to say: 'If ye love me, ye will keep my commandments' (John 14:15). This is the test of your love for Me, that you will do what I say. And what was that? It was to love the brethren even as He had loved them.

Then finally he remembered their *patience of hope*; that is, 'endurance inspired by hope' (N.I.V.). To be patient is to endure, to be steadfast, immoveable, in spite of all hardship, trial, or persecution. That quality of endurance was something his converts greatly needed, and he would have them know that its secret resides in the glorious certainties of hope. A faith which does not work would be lacking in credibility; a love which does not serve would be lacking in integrity; and a hope which does not endure would be lacking in reality. Hope is seen as the great motive force that sustains both faith and love; hope calls them both into action so that faith will wax more bold and love will grow in gladness. Such hope finds its centre 'in our Lord Jesus Christ, before our God and Father' (1:3). Perhaps there is no more noble definition of the meaning and place of such hope in our lives than in the words of a later benediction: 'Now our Lord Jesus Christ Himself, and God our Father which loved us and gave us eternal comfort and *good hope through grace*, comfort your hearts and stablish them in every good work and word' (2 Thess. 2:16-17). That hope draws all its strength from the fact that the Lord Himself dwells

in our hearts; the Christ who is in you is *the hope of glory* (Col.
1:27). Hope is objective in its character; it has an eye on the
Second Advent. It looks forward and waits 'for His Son from
heaven . . . even Jesus' (1:10). The skirl of the pipes that told the
beleaguered garrison of Lucknow that the Campbells were coming
confirmed their hope in the darkest hour that rescue was now at
hand. Just so, the great shout from heaven, the voice of the angel,
the sound of the trumpet, will bring our hope to its glorious
fruition (cf. 3:16). The Lord, 'even Jesus', shall come; and then?
Our feet shall stand within the gates of that glorious new Jerusalem; and our eyes shall behold the King in His beauty.

This remembrance was fortified with the assurance of the
sovereign favour of God: 'Knowing, brethren beloved of God,
your election' (1:4). That faith and love and hope represented the
strength of God's hold on their lives and gave sureness of knowledge and understanding as they thought of God's choice when
they were still far off from Him. They were addressed as those
who were *brethren* no less than twenty-one times in the course of
these two Letters. It was a small token of the bond of fellowship
and affection which bound them together in the Gospel: the great
Hebrew convert and his Gentile converts were 'one in Christ
Jesus' (Gal. 3:28). But they were not merely beloved by him;
they were *beloved of God*. God had set His heart on them with a
love that was everlasting; He had loved them while they were yet
sinners; His was a love that would not let them go. This was
manifest in their *election*. Gentiles, pagans, idolaters, they were
nevertheless beloved of God who had marked them out and
chosen them for Himself from all eternity. It was not their choice
of God that mattered; it was God's choice of them that had
brought them out of darkness into marvellous light. They might
trace God's work in their lives from that particular point in time
when they first heard the Gospel; that might be as far as they
could go in conscious recollection. They might recall how their
choice had been made, and they might think that that was the
moment when it all first began. But God's choice of them lay
behind their choice of God, and that was the ultimate proof that
the whole plan of salvation was of God, not of man. It was God

who had moved them to turn 'from idols to serve a living and true God' (1:9).

The most striking factor in this statement was Paul's certainty of their election; this was based on compelling evidence: 'How that our Gospel came not unto you in word only, but also in power, and in the Holy Ghost, and in much assurance' (1:5). He spoke of *our gospel*, pointing to 'the message rather than the act of preaching' (cf. 2 Thess. 2:14).[3] It was in fact God's great good news for all mankind, but he could speak of it in this context as *ours* because it was the great message from God in which he and they shared alike. That great good news had come to them through his ministry on his arrival in their city some months before; he had been the herald who had proclaimed that news for the first time in their hearing. That message was verbal in form; he had proclaimed it in words that made it articulate and intelligible. But it was *not in word only*; it was not the gift of eloquence nor the weight of argument on which he had sought to rely. That word had come *in power*; it was armed with divine authority. Paul may have felt that he spoke in weakness or fear or much trembling, but his words were transformed by the Spirit of God and were confirmed *in power*. They were 'the power of God unto salvation' for those who had believed (Rom. 1:16). That word had also come *in the Holy Ghost*; it had been in demonstration of the Spirit of God in power (cf. 1 Cor. 2:4). That was why it had been the means for a work of God in the souls of men; the Word of God and the Spirit of God were an irresistible combination. And that word had come as well *in much assurance*; he had proclaimed it with total conviction, and they had heard it with equal assurance. Therefore they could rejoice in the witness of God's Spirit with their spirit as to its truth, and relevance, and divine authority.

Paul ended this section with an appeal to the example which he and his companions had set: 'Even as ye know what manner of men we shewed ourselves toward you for your sake' (1:5). It is always impressive to observe the way in which Paul could appeal

---

[3] Leon Morris: The Epistles of Paul to The Thessalonians (*Tyndale Commentaries*) p. 37.

to his own example. This was never in a boastful, self-complacent spirit; it was always with an underlying vein of profound humility. It is self-evident in the affecting terms of his farewell to the elders of Ephesus: 'Ye yourselves know, from the first day that I set foot in Asia, after what manner I was with you all the time' (Acts 20:18). They knew, because they had observed his tears, his trials, and his testimony, and had been deeply moved as a result. To the troubled church at Corinth he could make the appeal: 'Be ye imitators of me, even as I also am of Christ' (1 Cor. 11:1). This is the more remarkable when it is placed beside the form which this exhortation took in another Epistle: 'Be ye therefore imitators of God, as beloved children' (Eph. 5:1). But he reverted to the example which his own life had set in yet another Epistle: 'Brethren, be ye imitators together of me, and mark them which so walk, even as ye have us for an ensample' (Phil. 3:17). The church is bound to rise or fall as the character of its ministers may rise or fall, and the ideal must be when its ministers can point to their character as an example for the church to imitate. It was in fact the clear light of God's grace in Paul's life that imbued his words with such authority, and his converts in turn 'became an ensample to all that believe in Macedonia and in Achaia' (1:7). Their own testimony was to reverberate through the hills and valleys of Greece until 'the word of the Lord' had sent its echo all over the country (1:8).[4]

---

[4] cf. J. R. W. Stott: Bible Reading at Keswick 1978. (see *The Gospel, The Spirit, The Church* p. 23).

Chapter Two

Not the Gospel of God Only

'We were well pleased to impart unto you, not the gospel
of God only, but also our own souls, because ye were
become very dear to us'.

1 THESSALONIANS 2:1-8

THE FIRST chapter reflects the confidence and affection of Paul
for his converts, and the great joy he felt that their testimony was
known throughout Macedonia and Achaia. It was common talk
among the churches in each Province that his visit to their city
had met with great blessing: 'For they themselves report concerning us what manner of entering in we had unto you; and how ye
turned unto God from idols, to serve a living and true God' (1:9).
The term *entering in* simply refers to them in that city; it was well
known how he had been received. Anyone at all, anywhere at all,
would be able to tell what was going on in Thessalonica. The first
verse in the next chapter takes up the same term and employs it
with a much wider significance: 'For yourselves, brethren, know
our *entering in* unto you, that it hath not been found vain' (2:1).
This not only spoke of his arrival and reception in their city, but
also of the influence of his ministry while he was there. What *they
themselves* (1:9), converts in the other churches, might have to say
was borne out by what *you yourselves* (2:1) know to be true. They
knew the kind of man he was; there was nothing to hide (cf. 1:5).
They could vividly remember how effective and manifest were
the results of his preaching. It was not a sorry failure; it had not
been in vain. There was nothing empty or aimless about his visit;
nothing merely ephemeral or superficial about his preaching. It
had led to an impressive and permanent change in their lives.
This was what had caught the notice of newly planted congrega-

tions in other cities; and it was the one thing which they knew for themselves, beyond doubt or question, as a fact in their own experience.

But the mention of his welcome in their midst led him to recall the grim circumstances which lay in the background: 'But having suffered before, and been shamefully entreated, as ye know, at Philippi, we waxed bold in our God to speak unto you the gospel of God in much conflict' (2:2). No single experience of persecution left so deep a scar on his mind as what befell him at Philippi, with the terrible exception of his being stoned at Lystra. He recalled that ordeal in a haunting sentence that can not be easily forgotten: 'From henceforth let no man trouble me: for I bear branded on my body the marks of Jesus' (Gal. 6:17). And at Philippi, he and Silas had been *shamefully entreated*. They had been seized and scourged, although neither tried nor condemned; they had been locked in the inmost prison, and their feet had been clamped in stocks. It was true that they had found grace to pray and sing hymns of praise at midnight, but these words tell in a poignant manner how terrible their sufferings had been. But they had no reason to be ashamed of their scars or imprisonment, for those weals on their backs had been incurred because of their testimony to Christ. The harsh effect of ill-treatment and of shameful indignity was still vivid in memory and emotion; and yet they had refused to be daunted and had *entered into* Thessalonica in order to begin again. They had *waxed bold* as they took up their task in what was still for them a new and strange city, and they had proved themselves fearless through the grace of God in preaching with a sense of complete freedom. Paul made it clear that what they had come to proclaim was *the Gospel of God* (cf. 1:5), and they did this in spite of *much conflict*. That phrase was the first hint of the Jewish opposition about which he would have much more to say.

But his first task was to embark on a detailed defence of motive and conduct: 'For our exhortation is not of error, nor of uncleanness, nor in guile' (2:3). This verse enters the text with an unexpected vigour at an unexpected moment, but it sprang from his hint about the *much conflict* in which he had become involved.

He had been the object of a sustained and vicious attack by Jewish leaders when they discovered that his ministry was as much for Gentiles as for themselves. They had provoked no small uproar and had driven him out of the city; their hostility had followed him to Beroea, and they were still intent on undermining his reputation by the use of slander. They had ascribed to him motives which could only deserve utter contempt, for in effect they said that he and his friends were no more than a group of religious charlatans. There were all too many people of this kind in an age when old creeds were crumbling under the assault of superstition. The Acts affords a glimpse into that strange world with pictures of Simon Magus, and Elymas the sorcerer, and the demon-possessed girl in the hands of a pitiless syndicate, and the seven sons of Sceva. But Paul vehemently denied that his preaching was motivated by worldly self-interest. His message had no truck with *error*; his methods were free from *guile*. The reference to *uncleanness* points to the Cabiric rites which were connected with Thessalonian culture and in which gross immorality was permitted, or promoted, with a religious sanction.[1] Nothing in Paul's preaching corresponded to such caricatures of all that was true and holy. He could only feel a burning indignation that *the Gospel of God* should be defamed by such accusations.

But he could not afford to let these character assassins have the last word and he at once went on to say: 'But even as we have been approved of God to be intrusted with the Gospel, so we speak; not as pleasing men, but God which proveth our hearts' (2:4). Those who traduced him were disowned in the strongest language, for his only concern was to please God without regard to the voice of slander. It is God who examines the heart to see whether its motives are genuine, and Paul was well aware that he had been subject to that test in its most searching spirit. He could only speak as he had spoken because he had been tried and was approved of God. As a result, he was allowed to be put in trust with, to become a trustee of, the Gospel. This was 'the gospel of the glory of the blessed God, which was committed to my trust' (1 Tim. 1:11). He saw himself as its appointed guardian; it was a

---

[1] J. B. Lightfoot: *Biblical Essays* p. 258.

trust which he held in a special sense on behalf of the Gentiles (cf. Gal. 2:7). It was for this reason that he declared himself in the emphatic assertion: *so we speak*. He was ever mindful of the transcendent character of the Gospel: therefore he did not preach himself; he could only proclaim Jesus as Lord (cf. 2 Cor. 4:5). There could be no question of his trying to adopt the tactics of a religious charlatan; his motives in preaching were as clear as crystal. 'We speak,' he said, 'not to please men, but to please God'. That set him free from the need to conform to the worldly pressures on a popular orator, and it taught him to fix his eyes on the standard which God Himself required. Therefore his one aim was to live for the glory of God, for God alone would try his heart and be his Judge. And that ought to have been the end of the matter.

But the end did not quite come at that point, for he turned to refute certain particular slanders: 'for neither at any time were we found using words of flattery, as ye know, nor a cloke of covetousness, God is witness' (2:5). He was still so deeply perturbed by the false and subtle innuendos which had been put into circulation that he felt he had to repudiate them in detail. Was he just a crowd-pleasing flatterer? His converts knew better. The word *flattery* does not represent the fair speech of a man who fawns on his hearers: it was more like cajolery, trying to lull people into a false sense of security. It was the glib smooth-tongued sales-talk of a professional con-man, the mark of the vagrant rhetoricians who were all out for their own ends. It was an age when strange sects of every conceivable kind sprang up and flourished exceedingly at the expense of well-meaning but ill-advised people; and the pity of it all was that those who got caught up with their speculations soon cut themselves off from the truth in its simplicity. Was he just a covetous self-seeker? He could call God as his witness. The *cloke* was 'a mask to cover up greed' (N.I.V.), and it suggests the suave kind of reason which is in fact no more than a pretext. It may seem plausible; it may sound persuasive; but it is not the truth. *Covetousness* is a term that includes any form of self-interest, any personal ambition, any spirit which is marked by the greed for more. Cajolery? *they* knew how he had warned them of imminent destruction (5:3). Covetousness? *God* knew that he would not allow himself to be a charge on them (2 Thess. 3:8). 'As you know, . . . as God is witness', all those ugly slanders were lies. (R.S.V.).

There were other slanders to the effect that all he sought for was human acclaim; he would vigorously repudiate such smears: 'Nor seeking glory of men, neither from you, nor from others, when we might have been burdensome, as apostles of Christ' (2:6). It could easily have been otherwise. There would have been a real burden on those hard-pressed converts if Paul and his friends had looked to them for material support. But that was not the case; they had refused to 'eat bread for nought at any man's hand' (2 Thess. 3:8). They had laboured night and day to earn their living that they 'might not burden' any of them (2 Thess. 3:8). The word *burdensome* is also translated in the Revised Version Margin by the phrase *claimed honour*, and that suggests a fresh meaning. They could have been *burdensome* if they had chosen to stand on privilege; they could have stood on their dignity as those who were *apostles of Christ*. This was what *might have been*; the element of temptation was recognised and rejected. They would not seek praise or honour, and they would not stand on their rights. They had never tried to divert notice from the Gospel in order to attract it to themselves. One of the most noble ministries in a land of noble ministries was that of Robert Murray McCheyne in Dundee. He was not quite thirty years old when he died in 1843, but he had long since come to the same mind as Paul in *not seeking glory* of men. 'I see a man can not be a faithful minister', he wrote, 'until he preaches Christ for Christ's sake; until he gives up striving to attract people to himself, and seeks only to attract them to Christ. Lord, give me this!'[2] And such a prayer would have become those who were *apostles of Christ*.

It was as though Paul felt that there had been enough of that as he now turned to make a strong affirmation about his own pastoral ministry: 'But we were gentle in the midst of you, as

[2] A. A. Bonar: *Memoir and Remains of the Rev. Robert Murray McCheyne*, p. 45.

when a nurse cherisheth her own children' (2:7). Paul had often spoken of his converts in terms of tenderness and affection; it was as though he could not find metaphors intimate enough for his purpose. He was *gentle* as one who would *cherish* a babe in arms. Each word helps to build up the thought of protective affection. The term *cherish* was a picture word which recalled how a bird would warm the chickens beneath her wings (cf. Matt. 23:37). He had acted like *a nurse* who would care for such babes as her own children. John Stott believes that the word *nurse* should be rendered *nursing mother*.[3]. This gains credence from yet another translation: 'We were gentle among you, like a *mother* caring for her little children' (N.I.V.). It is truly remarkable to see how a man like Paul could adopt such a delicate metaphor, but he carried it still further when he likened himself to a mother who had suffered the pangs of birth to bring forth her children. He even went beyond nature itself when he claimed that he had been in travail for his converts not once, but twice: 'My dear children, for whom I am *again* in the pains of childbirth until Christ is formed in you' (Gal. 4:19 N.I.V.). It was no less remarkable that within four verses he could move with perfect freedom to a second image and refer to himself as a *father*: 'Ye know how we dealt with each one of you, as a *father* with his own children' (2:11). And those parental metaphors would convey the realities of love and care better than any more elaborate statement he could devise.

This is heightened by a further declaration of his love and longing for them: 'Even so, being affectionately desirous of you, we were well pleased to impart unto you, not the gospel of God only, but also our own souls, because ye were become very dear to us' (2:8). The term *affectionately desirous* is an uncommon expression, derived from a fairly rare word. Was it perhaps an expression of endearment derived from the nursery? Did it hold some nostalgic memory for Paul as he thought of his own childhood? At all events, it helped him to declare his love for them and to say how gladly he would impart to them

[3] cf. J. R. W. Stott, *ibid*. p. 31.

much more than the Gospel. They would have given even *our own selves* (R.S.V.); there was nothing they wanted to withhold. This was a strong personal expression for self-giving, and is illustrated by his comment on the generous attitude of the Philippian congregation: 'First they gave *their own selves* to the Lord, and to us by the will of God' (2 Cor. 8:5). This was in the very spirit of Christ who came into the world, loving, giving, serving, saving; it was derived from God Himself who did not spare even His Son but gave Him for us all. And what prompted Paul to write in such terms? It was because they had become *very dear* to his heart. There was nothing here of clinical detachment; there was rather a strong sense of personal involvement. Paul could never detach himself from his converts because they were in his heart to live or to die with him (cf. 2 Cor. 7:3). Few words better describe what should be the ideal pattern for the mutual relations of pastor and people. The churches of Macedonia held a unique place in his heart; he wrote of them as of no church besides: 'What is our hope, or joy, or crown of glorying? Are not even ye before our Lord Jesus at his coming? For ye are our glory and our joy' (2:19-20: cf. Phil. 4:1).

Chapter Three

For Now We Live, if Ye Stand Fast

'For what thanksgiving can we render again unto God for you, for all the joy wherewith we joy for your sakes before our God?'

1 THESSALONIANS 3:1-10

PAUL'S MIND constantly reverted to the circumstances which had forced him to leave Thessalonica. The wrench from his converts in that idolatrous city had been for him a most painful deprivation. His heart was still with them; they were never far from his mind. He still longed to return; indeed he had planned to do so more than once. But his plans had not worked out: 'Satan hindered us' (2:18). We do not know what that brief and cryptic statement implies, though its meaning may have been clear enough to his readers. He had encountered obstacles which had made a return visit impossible, and he felt that this was Satan at work. But his anxiety for their welfare increased until it was barely tolerable. He had gone as far as Beroea where he found that the Jews 'were more noble than those in Thessalonica, in that they received the word with all readiness of mind, examining the scriptures daily, whether these things were so' (Acts 17:11). But when the Jews of Thessalonica heard that he was in Beroea, they sent some of their own number to stir up fresh trouble. Paul's life was in danger, and once more he had to fall back on the alternative of flight. 'Immediately the brethren sent forth Paul to go as far as to the sea: but Silas and Timothy abode there still' (Acts 17:14). Those unnamed local friends accompanied him as far

15

as Athens where he proposed to wait until Silas and Timothy could re-join him. He was lonely, dispirited, and above all, desperately anxious for news of his converts. 'Wherefore', he wrote, 'when we could no longer forbear, we thought it good to be left behind at Athens alone' (3:1). His own need for companionship would take second place to his deep concern for the church in Thessalonica, and he resolved to remain in Athens alone so that Timothy could visit his converts in that city.

His companions from Beroea would convey this message for Timothy on their return from Athens: 'We . . . sent Timothy, our brother and God's minister in the gospel of Christ, to establish you and to comfort you concerning your faith; that no man be moved by these afflictions; for yourselves know that hereunto we are appointed' (3:2-3). It would seem that Silas was to continue in Beroea while Timothy back-tracked to Thessalonica: he was to do what Paul and Barnabas had done when they returned to Lystra and Iconium and Antioch, where the Jews had lately sought to kill them (Acts 14:21). Timothy himself was a convert of that missionary journey, and Paul spoke of him in terms which indicate his deep affection. He spoke of him as a brother beloved and a valued servant of the Gospel or 'a fellow worker with God' (R.V.M.). Timothy was still a young man and this was his first independent mission. Why did Paul choose Timothy rather than Silas for this hazardous enterprise? Paul and Silas had been coupled in suffering at Philippi (Acts 16:19); it was Paul and Silas who had been in special danger in Thessalonica (Acts 17:10). Timothy was therefore the obvious choice for such a purpose; he was the least likely of the three to attract notice from a hostile quarter. His task was clear: he was to establish and encourage the church in faith. He had come out of a background in which persecution had been severe; what God had done for him, He was more than able to do for them. He had learned from experience what it meant to stand fast in the trial of his faith. Therefore he could win their confidence by his testimony and build them up in faith lest they should be *unsettled* as a result of trial (N.I.V.). They would discover that trial was their destiny as sons of God in a runaway world.

Paul had warned them in advance that tribulation would come as part of God's purpose: 'For verily, when we were with you, we told you beforehand that we are to suffer affliction; even as it came to pass, and ye know' (3:4). These words were not written by a man who had a persecution complex, but he had had enough experience to know that those who tried to live for Christ would meet hostility. He had come to them as one who had been 'shamefully entreated' (2:2), and they knew all too well how he had been hounded out of their own city. He had repeatedly warned them of the risk of persecution, and his warnings had been fulfilled in a dramatic upheaval. In his own case, the Jews had been the chief agents in the persecution he had endured, and there are signs in these Letters that his good-will for the Jews had been strained almost beyond the point that he could bear. But he never forgot that he was born a Jew and his love for his own people outlived all the hurt and indignation which they had caused. Gentile cynics in a later age would mock and deride the Jews:

> How odd of God
> To choose the Jews!

Paul would never subscribe to that frivolous sentiment; nor would he have cared to sponsor the couplet in reply:

> But not so odd as those who choose
> A Jewish God, and hate the Jews.

Perhaps it was at the hands of Gentiles that his readers were to suffer, not at the hands of Jews. But in either case, his words seem to go beyond an expectation of hostility; they imply that suffering is an essential element in the experience of a believer.

Paul went on to reiterate what he had said at the very outset: 'For this cause I also, when I could no longer forbear, sent that I might know your faith, lest by any means the tempter had tempted you, and our labour should be in vain' (3:5). Paul had diverged slightly from the main line of thought in order to remind them how he had warned them in advance of persecution to come. Now he resumed the thread of thought with which he had begun, and the phrase *for this cause* corresponds with the word *wherefore* in the first verse. This was followed by the further declaration that he could *no longer forbear*, and the only difference was his choice of the singular pronoun rather than the plural. This may suggest that there was an increasing emphasis on his sense of personal urgency. He had sent to find out whether their faith had been equal to the test of persecution and he longed to know that they had not been shaken in that crisis. It was not so much that he stood in doubt; but he knew what such trials were like. He knew that *the tempter* had put them to the test, and that test must have proved whether or not his work had been in vain. The *tempter* was none other than *Satan* who had hindered him from coming (cf. 2:18). Just as Satan had blocked his path, so he would have tried them to the uttermost. Paul longed for the reassurance that their faith had endured. It was so much easier to tolerate the loneliness which he felt in Athens than to bear the suspense while he waited for news. It was one thing for him to have suffered persecution on their account; it was totally different for his converts to be exposed to that kind of tribulation. He had to preach; he had to call them to believe; and he had to do it even though he knew that it would expose them to violence or cruelty or suffering.

It was because he felt responsible for the fact that they were exposed to that ordeal that he was so enormously relieved when good news came to him at last: 'But when Timothy came even now unto us from you, and brought us glad tidings of your faith and love, and that ye have good remembrance of us always, longing to see us, even as we also to see you' (3:6). Paul had left Athens and gone to Corinth before Silas and Timothy could rejoin him, but he wrote this Letter while the first flush of joy at their coming was at its peak. Timothy's arrival was so recent that his cup was filled to the brim, for the news he had brought was such as to invigorate him with a new strength of purpose. It was clear from The Acts that his ministry in Corinth sprang to life with a new spur of drive and dedication: 'When Silas and Timothy came down from Macedonia, Paul was constrained by the word, testifying to the Jews that Jesus was the Christ' (Acts 18:5). They brought *good news* (N.I.V.); and this is the only verse where this word is used for something other than *the Gospel of Christ* (3:2; cf. 2:2, 8, 9). To hear of their *faith and love* gave him the solid reassurance for which he longed: their *faith* had come through fire, and their *love* was still in full flower. Nor was that all, because he had been told as well of their continued loyalty and their personal devotion to him. It had been of primary importance to learn that they had proved steadfast in faith; but he was too human not to rejoice that their love for him was undiminished. They longed to see him just as much as he longed to see them, and the cumulative effect of such good news filled his heart with overwhelming gladness. It was in the strength of such ties that the secret of his amazing ministry in large measure was found; 'anxiety for all the churches' was based on an unbounded affection for each and all his converts (2 Cor. 11:28).

Paul found that he could not let this theme go without a more ample reference: 'For this cause, brethren, we were comforted over you in all our distress and affliction through your faith: for now we live, if ye stand fast in the Lord' (3:7-8). The phrase *for this cause* is an echo of the earlier expression (3:5; cf. 3:1). When he could no longer contain his anxiety and suspense, he had sent to find out the real state of affairs, and the report he had received was such as to gladden his heart with praise. It was *this cause* that he had kept in mind, and it was still in mind as he called them *brethren*. He had found fresh encouragement and strength for his own soul at the news of their faith; it had helped to render his own immediate *distress and affliction* tolerable. The Acts affords little more than a hint of this overwhelming pressure, but it is clear that when he left Athens, he had felt like a man who was almost crushed in spirit. Then this good news had come; he was transformed. It is as though his words were a window through which we look into his very soul: 'For now we live, if ye stand fast in the Lord'. The word *now* means that as he wrote, his heart throbbed with the pulse of life; he had been brought back as it were from the edge of the grave that he might *live*. He was bound up in the bundle of life with them; he could only *live* while they stood fast in the Lord. That is why the pronoun *ye* is in an emphatic position; theirs had been a test case for him. Could those converts who had turned from idols to the true and living God survive when persecuted? They could; and their steadfast faith had vindicated both his ministry and his confidence.

Then in accord with his custom, he turned from his converts to God Himself: 'For what thanksgiving can we render again unto God for you, for all the joy wherewith we joy for your sakes before our God?' (3:9). The question was rhetorical; no real answer could be furnished. How could he thank God enough for all that He had done? The whole Letter was in fact full of thanksgiving. He had begun with the generous expression of a grateful heart as he was put in mind of their faith and love and hope; 'We give thanks to God always for you all, making mention of you in our prayers' (1:2). He caught up the same theme when he came to speak of their warm response to his preaching: 'We also thank God without ceasing that when ye received from us the word of the message, ... ye accepted it not as the word of men, but, as it is in truth, the word of God' (2:13). Now he asked how he could ever be too thankful for the knowledge that their faith had proved so strong and reliable even in the fire of persecution. On the human level, it might have seemed as though their faith were a triumph for him; but he took no credit at all for the triumph of God's grace in the heart of his converts. He could only ascribe glory to God for their steadfast faith and obedience; it had brought him untold joy for their sakes in the presence of God. The way in which he spoke of that joy was like an echo of the earlier utterance: 'What is our hope, or *joy*, or crown of glorying? Are not even *ye*?' (2:19). These converts in Thessalonica were his glory and joy: his glory, because he could honour them in the hearing of others; his joy, because they filled his heart with praise in the presence of God. He could truly say of them as of few besides: 'I joy, and rejoice with you all' (Phil. 2:17).

Paul ended this passage with the fervent hope that he would see them again: 'Night and day praying exceedingly that we may see your face, and may perfect that which is lacking in your faith' (3:10). Paul was forced to struggle for words that would adequately express all that was in his heart. He felt a deep, persistent nostalgia for them that found relief only as he prayed *night and day*. Nor was that all, because he went on to say that he prayed *exceedingly*. This word is a double compound; it is only found twice in his writings elsewhere. He could exhort his converts to esteem those who were set over them 'in the Lord *exceeding highly* in love for their work's sake' (5:13). He could commend them to God as the One who is 'able to do *exceeding abundantly* above all that we ask or think' (Eph. 3:20). So in this verse, the word gives the idea of the *exceeding abundant* desire that made him long to see their face. But while he gave full rein to his longing for them and his joy in their faith, he longed as well that he might be able to make up that which was lacking in their experience of faith. This phrase may be compared with a yet more personal expression of longing and desire: 'Now I rejoice in my sufferings for your sake, and fill up on my part that which is *lacking* of the afflictions of Christ in my flesh for his body's sake, which is the church' (Col. 1:24). He was not blind to the fact that their faith was still far from perfect; there was still much that was *lacking*, that fell short or that came behind, in the standard of full maturity. Therefore Paul the evangelist began to merge into Paul the pastor as he longed to confirm their hearts 'unblameable in holiness before our God and Father at the coming of our Lord Jesus' (3:13).

Chapter Four

In Holiness and Honour

'We beseech and exhort you in the Lord Jesus, that, as ye
received of us how ye ought to walk and to please God,
even as ye do walk, – that ye abound more and more'.
                                              1 THESSALONIANS 4:1-8

THIS SHORT Letter begins to move towards its close with an
exhortation to right living: 'Finally then, brethren, we beseech
and exhort you in the Lord Jesus, that as ye received of us how
ye ought to walk and to please God, even as ye do walk, – that
ye abound more and more' (4:1). No doubt what he meant to
say was inspired by what he had heard from Timothy; but he
did not intend to say anything which they had not heard
before. No less than four verses in this passage refer to the
teaching he had given them on moral questions while he had
been with them. He would remind them of the charge he had
sought to lay on mind and conscience, and he renewed it in
terms that combined the two key-notes of tenderness and
urgency. He would ask or beseech; he would urge or exhort;
but he would speak only in the Name of the Lord Jesus. This
was basic to all that he might have to say; he spoke in view of
their union with each other which in turn grew out of union
with Him. This made it as clear as crystal that he did not try
to speak on his own authority; they had *received* from him only
what he had first received from God. The word *received* was
almost a technical expression and was used to mark their
response to the Gospel. It points to the primitive tradition
handed down from the Lord Jesus through His servants to
people like themselves. 'Ye *received* from us the word of the
message, even the word of God' (2:13); 'ye *accepted* it, not as

22

the word of men, but as it is in truth, the word of God' (2:13). It was the hard core of apostolic testimony to Christ which made up Paul's missionary teaching, and they were to *abound* in understanding and obedience more and yet more.

One phrase at the heart of this verse calls for special notice: 'how ye ought to walk and to please God'. No formula for holiness is so clear as this luminous and lovely phrase; no definition in theology can improve this statement of the practical evidence of a truly sanctified life. God walked in the garden in the cool of the day before sin came into the world, calling Adam into communion and fellowship with Himself (Gen. 3:8). Adam lost that amazing privilege as a result of sin, but the original ideal was wonderfully exemplified in the life and character of Enoch. This was represented in the Old Testament by the word *walk* and in the New Testament by the phrase *to please God*. It was written of him in the history of the patriarchs: 'Enoch walked with God: and he was not; for God took him' (Gen. 5:24). And this corresponds with the record in the catalogue of those who were valiant in faith: 'Before his translation, he had this testimony, that he pleased God' (Heb. 11:5 A.V.). *To walk* implies both purpose and progress; it is not to stroll or saunter without any clear aim or goal. To walk *with God* is so to live that God Himself may be well pleased; it was in this sense that Enoch, Noah and Abraham were all said to have walked with God (Gen. 5:24; 6:9; 17:1). *To please God* is so to live that all our ways are ordered as in God's sight; it is to be like Christ who did not seek to please Himself, but did always those things which pleased His Father (Rom. 15:3; John 8:29). This is how those who are sons of God ought to live; 'not as pleasing men, but God which proveth our hearts' (1 Thess. 2:4). This is not a matter which is left for our choice; it is not an option of more or less indifferent value. It is like a divine imperative, and from that there is no escape.

Paul went on to remind them of what they had heard before: 'For ye know what charge we gave you through the Lord Jesus: for this is the will of God, even your sanctification' (4:2-3). Paul had never tried to impose his own ideals or standards on others; what he had set before them were divine commands in the Name of the Lord Jesus. The whole matter was placed on the highest level when he referred it to *the will of God*. He would use a similar dogmatic preface when he called them to be thankful: 'In everything give thanks: for this is *the will of God* in Christ Jesus to you-ward' (5:18). There could be no higher point of reference; it set the tone for all he had to say. And what the will of God demands is summed up in one phrase of great spiritual significance: it is *even your sanctification*. This was not a question of doctrine; he was concerned with the sober realities of conduct. Sanctification is as necessary for a convert to Christ as is Justification for a sinner; the one grows out of the other. The man who has been justified on the ground that Christ was *for* him in His death on the cross must go on to be sanctified in view of the fact that Christ is *in* him as the ever-living Saviour. Sanctification is therefore the process by which imperfect believers are made holy. This is something that will result in a change of character, and it must be progressive. It is true that *holiness* is a word that has gone out of fashion in our modern society; it is seldom used in ordinary conversation today. This means that it will not be long before people are no longer sure what it means; but its meaning can be expressed in a very simple statement. To be holy is to become like Christ; to be Christ-like; to grow into the kind of man God wants to see. And this is *sanctification*.

But this exhortation was quite explicit; it applied to sexual purity: 'For this is the will of God, even your sanctification, that ye abstain from fornication; that each of you know how to possess himself of his own vessel in sanctification and honour' (4:3-4). One of the worst features in the culture of Greece and Rome was their sexual laxity. As a result, early converts to Christ came out of a permissive, sex-ridden society which saw no wrong in all kinds of moral licence. They found it hard to feel deeply on a matter which had always been part of their environment. It was a mark of Paul's understanding of the situation that he grappled with it from the very start so firmly: he made no concession; there was no compromise. At that very moment he was living in Corinth where the worship of Aphrodite dominated the city; and he was writing to the church in Thessalonica where the sensual religious rites of the Cabiri were a controlling influence in the lives of ordinary people. He could hardly avoid the duty that required him to provide definite instruction on such matters. So he began with a negative direction; the will of God required a clean break from all forms of immorality: fornication, adultery, or any other aberration to which the Greek word might apply. Then he rephrased the thought with a positive emphasis; the will of God required them to learn self-control: they were to keep themselves pure. He may have used the word *vessel* as a euphemism for a *wife*, but this is improbable (cf. R.S.V.). It seems to have been an image for the *body* (cf. 2 Cor. 4:7); it may have had a more particular meaning (cf. 1 Sam. 21:5). But the object is clear: casual relations in the realm of sex should have no place in their lives. 'Each of you should learn to control his own body in a way that is holy and honourable' (N.I.V.).

In the absence of a connecting particle, the next words must be read as a further comment: 'Not in the passion of lust, even as the Gentiles which know not God' (4:5). The combination of *passion* and *lust* is of more than transient interest, because the phrase throws light on the psychology of temptation. The word *lust* in itself simply refers to strong desire, but it is used nearly always in a bad sense. The word *passion* refers to that kind of inward feeling by which a man may be overmastered. *Lust* may respond to an external temptation; *passion* is the habit which indulgence of temptation creates. Both ideas are combined in this verse with singular emphasis: 'Not in passionate lust like the heathen, who do not know God' (N.I.V.). They were never to regard the body merely as an instrument for self-indulgence; true self-control will never permit the surrender of a man to his own passions. Any failure in this respect wears the stamp and image of sin; it is to do *even as the Gentiles* who spent their lives in the darkest idolatry. The word *Gentiles* did not mark them out as distinct from Jews; it referred to pagans as

distinct from converts to Christ. Paul felt this so strongly that
he applied the same thought in striking language elsewhere:
'This I say therefore, and testify in the Lord, that ye no longer
walk *as the Gentiles* also walk' (Eph. 4:17). Gentiles, absorbed
in a world of pagan idolatry, did not know God; they were like
all those who reject such light as they could have, and so choose
to live in darkness. The most frightening description of the
Gentile world in Paul's day is set out in the first chapter of his
Letter to The Romans. When men chose to turn their back on
God, God gave them up; they were left in the mire of lusts
that were as vile as they were unnatural.

There is no shift in the main line of thought as Paul pursues
this theme: 'That no man transgress and wrong his brother in
the matter: because the Lord is an avenger in all these things,
as also we forewarned you and testified' (4:6). The phrase *in the
matter* is well enough explained by the context; it is expressed
like this from a sense of delicacy. Sexual sin can not be
overlooked as if it were no more than a private matter; it has
social repercussions. No one can break the law of God *in this
matter* (N.I.V.) without also in some respect cheating others. It
not only undermines holiness; it not only destroys a man's
honour; it affects our *brother*. The wrong use of the sex instinct
wrongs our *brother*; that is, our fellow man. It is to *go beyond*
(A.V.) or *transgress* the proper limits of conduct and freedom; it
is to *defraud* (A.V.) or *wrong* some other person by an act of
dishonesty at his or her expense. The fraud consists in the fact
that it treats someone else as having less than a true share of
personal dignity. Therefore Paul went on to add a salutary
warning that ought to ring in the ears of western society today:
'the Lord is an *avenger* in all these things'. The same word is
used in another Epistle to enforce the authority of earthly rulers
as God's servants: such a magistrate is 'an *avenger* for wrath to
him that doeth evil' (Rom. 13:4). God will call for justice *in
all these things*, whether fornication, or adultery, or any deviation
into what is vile and unnatural. Paul had solemnly testified to
this effect while he was still with them; he had *forewarned* them
in terms that pointed right on to the day of judgment. They

had heard the voice of conscience, that still small voice that makes one feel smaller still; it was a summons so to order their lives that they would not be put to shame on that great day.

This strong exhortation drew strength from a recollection of the original purpose of their calling: 'For God called us not for uncleanness, but in sanctification' (4:7). A vocation to *uncleanness* as a way of life was the lot of the vestal virgins in the temple of Aphrodite at Corinth, but the God who is our Father has not so called any of us. No, by no means; because passion and lust only serve to destroy human integrity, human community, and human personality. The wrong done to others in broken homes, unwanted pregnancies, and illegitimate children; or in emotional distress, weakened moral fibre, and loss of self-respect, can never be calculated. Therefore any misuse of this instinct must be seen as unclean; it has no place in God's purpose; it gives rise to complications which can not be foreseen.[1] Therefore God's call is of primary importance for all who will obey. It is a call to be holy; to be totally committed to live for His glory. For the third time in this passage, Paul speaks of *sanctification* (cf. 4:3, 4); and the change of preposition from *for* to *in* indicates that such holiness was to be the very atmosphere in which their lives would move. Did he set too high a standard or ask too much of his converts? 'Be not deceived', he would tell the church at Corinth; 'neither fornicators, nor idolaters, nor adulterers, nor effeminate, nor abusers of themselves with men . . . shall inherit the kingdom of God. *And such were some of you:* but ye were washed, but ye were sanctified, but ye were justified in the name of the Lord Jesus Christ, and in the Spirit of our God' (1 Cor. 6:9-11). And that astonishing change in the lives of such people was the finest demonstration that the Gospel is the power of God to save those who will only believe.

The whole exhortation comes to an end with a very solemn warning: 'Therefore he that rejecteth, rejecteth not man, but God, who giveth his Holy Spirit unto you' (4:8). This brief statement is the logical conclusion: to reject this word is to

[1] cf. William Neil: *St. Paul's Epistles To the Thessalonians.* p. 76.

reject God Himself. It would matter little to Paul if they were to reject him as a man, but to reject God should have been unthinkable. That is why he strove to make them see that sexual laxity is more than an offence against a *brother* or society as such. It is to treat God as though God can be ignored, disregarded, because it is a slur on the image of God in which each of us has been made. This is carried to the ultimate point of argument in the last clause; it is a sin against God who gave us no less a gift than His Holy Spirit. This gift placed them in a different position from that which they had held before; it marked them off from the old world which was submerged in paganism and idolatry. It gave them an inner witness against all that was unclean or impure, and that witness was ever being renewed by God's continuous process of giving. No one can lift himself by his own shoe laces to a higher level than that on which he stands; nor can we lift ourselves by our own self-effort to a spiritual level that was beyond our reach before. But what we can not do in our own strength, God is able to do in and for us through His Holy Spirit who is given for this very purpose. 'Know ye not that ye are a temple of God, and that the Spirit of God dwelleth in you?' (1 Cor. 3:16). 'Know ye not that your body is a temple of the Holy Ghost which is in you?' (1 Cor. 6:19). *Therefore*, so Paul argued, he that rejects this word must be seen as guilty before the God who gives us His Spirit; and he that destroys the temple of God, him shall God destroy (1 Cor. 3:17).

Chapter Five

Sons of the Day

'So then let us not sleep, as do the rest, but let us watch
and be sober'.

1 THESSALONIANS 5:1-10

PAUL TOOK up one special problem in this passage as the Letter
moved to an end: this had to do with the Second Coming of
the Lord Jesus. It is clear that Timothy must have reported
certain flaws in faith and conduct on the part of these new
converts. There was something lacking in their faith which
Paul longed to perfect or supply (3:10). There was need for
him to exhort them to make it their aim to live quietly and
work diligently (4:11). Some were disorderly; others were faint-
hearted; a few were weak (5:14). Paul had something appropriate in the way of caution or of comfort for each and all. But
the dominating issues were all wrapped up with the Second
Coming; they had been drawn into a whole network of quite
needless anxieties as they contemplated the shape of things to
come. What would become of those who died before the Lord's
return? How could they tell when the end would occur? And
how would all these things affect their hope? But Paul would
not indulge in a profitless discussion about times and seasons.
He had dealt with this when he had been in their midst and he
would not repeat what he had said before: 'But concerning the
times and the seasons, brethren, ye have no need that aught be
written unto you' (5:1). The word *times* points to the date when
this great event will come to pass; the word *seasons* points to the
signs that will mark its approach.[1] Jesus Himself had said that

[1] J. B. Lightfoot: *Notes on Epistles of St. Paul* from *Unpublished Commentaries*. p.
71.

29

no one could foretell that day or hour; it was something which
not even the Son of Man had within His human knowledge
(Mark 13:32). One of His last sayings before the Ascension
from Olivet had been explicit: 'It is not for you to know times
or seasons which the Father hath set within his own authority'
(Acts 1:7). Paul had nothing further to say on that subject.

They ought to have furnished their own answer to those
questions from what they knew: 'For yourselves know perfectly
that the day of the Lord so cometh as a thief in the night' (5:2).
The word *perfectly* suggests that there was nothing to add to
what he had told them; it may even be a hint that there was
nothing to add to what Jesus had said (cf. Matt. 24:43; Luke
12:39). *The Day of The Lord* was a phrase that went back to the
prophets: it was used by them to designate the time when
God's sovereign control would be manifest in the overthrow of
His enemies (cf. Isa. 2:12; Jer. 46:10; Ezek. 7:10). It was
applied in a special manner to the day of judgment of which
lesser visitations were no more than a type.[2] That day *cometh*;
and the present tense makes it so much more vivid, although
it is meant to denote the certainty of arrival rather than its
nearness in point of time.[3] It comes *as a thief in the night*; it
comes by stealth, and its coming will be swift and unexpected
like that of a thief who moves in the dark. The Lord Jesus had
warned the Twelve to be on the alert because they did not
know the day when He would come: 'But know this, that if the
master of the house had known in what watch the thief was
coming, he would have watched and would not have suffered
his house to be broken through' (Matt. 24:43). The man who
trusts in the security of locks is caught unawares when an
intruder breaks in; for the thief comes by night and in stealth
to spring a surprise. So it will be with the day of judgment:
'The day of the Lord will come as a thief (2 Pet. 3:10). It will
come at a time when men are least prepared.

Those who ought to have most cause for concern will be the
least apprehensive: 'When they are saying, Peace and safety,

[2] J. B. Lightfoot, *ibid.* p. 71.
[3] Ibid.

then sudden destruction cometh upon them, as travail upon a woman with child; and they shall in no wise escape' (5:3). This verse is so markedly different in style from his normal usage that it demands recognition; it is as though we had stumbled on a passage from the prophets.[4]. There have always been false prophets ready to cry *peace and safety*. Jeremiah had declared: 'They have healed also the hurt of my people lightly, saying, Peace, peace; when there is no peace' (Jer. 6:14). Ezekiel had accused: 'They have seduced my people, saying, Peace; and there is no peace' (Ezek. 13:10). But the crack of doom will thunder in the ears of all who dwell in that false security; *sudden destruction* will overtake them. This will be as certain and as sudden as the pangs of child-birth; it will come *as travail upon a woman with child*. There is no warning in the case of a thief in the night; there is no escape in the case of a woman in labour. The first signs of travail may come prematurely when it is least convenient for the woman herself; nevertheless when they begin, the result is inevitable; there can be no escape and no delay. The Lord Jesus had forewarned the disciples that certain things would mark 'the beginning of travail' (Mark 13:8); and when travail begins, it goes on to the end. So it will be with that day of judgment. People will be immersed in the 'cares of this life' and that day will close on them like a trap (Luke 21:34). Nothing could be clearer than His counsel if they were not to be overwhelmed unawares: 'Watch ye at every season, making supplication that ye may prevail to escape all these things that shall come to pass' (Luke 21:36).

But the prospect before those who believe is in total contrast with that of the unbeliever: 'But ye, brethren, are not in darkness, that that day should overtake you as a thief' (5:4). The *ye* is emphatic; they had been brought out of darkness to stand in the sunlight of His glorious promises. The same ring of personal emphasis is seen in the contrast between those who were still darkened in their understanding and those who had passed from darkness into the light: *They* were now past feeling, 'but *ye* did not so learn Christ' (Eph. 4:20). So Paul

[4] cf. Lightfoot, *ibid*. p. 72.

said that because they were *not in darkness*, they ought to be prepared for the coming of that great day. He continued the metaphor of the thief who comes in the night; but this was to argue that those who no longer dwell in darkness are not afraid of thieves. They should not be caught by surprise; they know what to expect. Then a little word-play allowed him to move from *that day* to a fresh line of thought: 'For ye are all sons of light, and sons of the day: we are not of the night, nor of darkness' (5:5). This verse illustrates the figure of speech known as chiasm as well as the balance of ideas in the apostle's argument. *Light* is in contrast with *darkness*; *day* is in contrast with *night*; and this diagonal correspondence helps to create a strong overall impression. Those who are *sons* reflect the quality and character of their parents. So the *sons of light* must have light as their hall-mark; they do not dwell in darkness. *Sons of the day* belong to the region where light has come; they do not belong to the night. Paul then identified himself with his readers by the sudden change of pronoun from *ye* to *we*; we who believe have now come out of the sphere of night and darkness into the light that Christ alone affords.

Those who are sons of light have no cause for self-indulgent complacency: 'So then, let us not sleep, as do the rest, but let us watch and be sober' (5:6). The main reason why the burglar takes people by surprise is that he comes by night; they are asleep, out of action, and off their guard. To drowse and dream is the condition natural to those who are sons of the night; to sleep is what we would expect in the case of those who dwell in darkness. *So then*, Paul went on to argue, it was not for him nor for his converts to be caught in that state; they ought not to do *as do the rest* (cf. 4:5). They were to bear in mind the fact that the birth-pangs of a new age have come; that new day has begun to dawn. Therefore their great need was to be awake, with their eyes wide open and with their minds on the alert. They were to *watch*, which would imply spiritual vigilance; they were to be *sober*, which would demand moral emphasis. And why? 'For they that sleep sleep in the night; and they that be drunken are drunken in the night' (5:7). This was not another metaphor; it was a factual argument; night is the time when men go to sleep or when they get drunk. But it grew out of the preceding metaphor and lends itself to a development of the same theme. The word *sleep* is used in the sense of a sleeping conscience; it is applied to the careless and indifferent. Getting *drunk* is used in the sense of irresponsible conduct; it is applied to the reckless and profligate.[5] It was not as though Paul's converts had failed to watch or were prone to drunkenness; they had learned not to live *as the Gentiles* who were without the true knowledge of God (4:5). Nevertheless they would always need to cultivate temperance, to avoid all excess, if they were to walk as sons of the day.

Paul pursued the contrast with a renewed summons for a sober spirit: 'But let us, since we are of the day, be sober, putting on the breastplate of faith and love; and for a helmet, the hope of salvation' (5:8). There is a certain overlap between night and day: 'The darkness is passing away, and the true light already shineth' (1 John 2:8). But we are of *the day*; therefore we ought to be *sober*: and this is in contrast with those who are drunk in the night. Perhaps the reference to vigilance would prompt the next idea of a soldier; he passed at once to the picture of a sentry armed and on guard. There would be a similar transition in a famous passage elsewhere: 'The night is far spent, and the day is at hand: let us therefore cast off the works of darkness, and let us put on the armour of light' (Rom. 13:12). Imagery of this kind had a strong fascination for Paul who came to know much of Roman soldiers (2 Cor. 6:7; 10:4; Eph. 6:11-18). The details of armour or of weapons varied from time to time, but they always lent themselves to picture language. Here Paul confines himself to the *breastplate* and the *helmet* in language that recalls the words of the prophet: 'And he put on righteousness as a breastplate, and an helmet of salvation upon his head' (Isa. 59:17). Here *faith* and *love* take the place of *righteousness* as the *breastplate*, and the *helmet* is not simply *salvation*, but *the hope of salvation* (cf. Eph. 6:14, 17). Salvation is an inclusive term that takes in the whole of Christ's

[5] cf. William Neil. *ibid.* p. 106; J. B. Lightfoot, *ibid.* p. 75.

work for His people; but the emphasis on *hope* marks the character of what is still to come. Leaving aside the pieces of armour, we fix our eyes on the realities for which they stand, and here we find *faith* and *love* and *hope* in the same order as before (cf. 1:3).

Paul went on to state the reason why we have cause for hope, and none for fear: 'For God appointed us not unto wrath, but unto the obtaining of salvation through our Lord Jesus Christ' (5:9). It is God who acted to save us from the wrath that sin deserves. He took the first great step to meet us in our need; all that He has done for us must be seen as the grace of God in action. He saved us from 'the wrath to come' (1:10), and that wrath must not be taken lightly. Paul had also spoken of those who fill up their own cup of sin: 'the wrath is come upon them to the uttermost' (2:16). The wrath of God is not some blind emotional force that is loosed against evil-doers; it is the just retribution which must descend on those who break His law. Nothing should be allowed to reduce our understanding of the terrible character of the wrath that belongs to God; that could only reduce our idea of the serious character of the salvation He has provided. We were rescued from wrath so that we might obtain that salvation; God in His great mercy chose us when we deserved nothing but wrath and saved us 'through our Lord, even Jesus, the Christ'. It was as though Paul could never remind them too often of what they owed to the mighty Saviour whose Name he had proclaimed. There was rescue; there was escape; there was deliverance from wrath: they had been saved when that must have seemed as though it were beyond all hope; and that had been because of Christ, and Christ alone. So the imagery of day and night, of breastplate and helmet, came to an end in a luminous conclusion that would fasten their eyes on the Person of Christ. He came into the world to save, to save sinners. It is Jesus alone who can rescue Gentile and Jew alike from the wrath they deserve.

Paul summed up all that Christ has done for us in one crisp sentence: 'Who died for us, that, whether we wake or sleep, we should live together with him' (5:10). This is the only verse in

this Letter in which the death of Christ is brought to our notice
as the ground on which our salvation was obtained. It may
seem strange that Paul did not link it with the Resurrection
(cf. 4:14); he was content in this case to refer to the fact that
He *died for us*, on our behalf, because this lay at the heart of
apostolic testimony. He went on to expand what this implies
by showing its purpose for those who have been brought into
union with Him. He *died* for us so that we may *live* with Him;
His death was the ground from which our life now springs.
And that is true *whether we wake or sleep*, whether we live or die.
He had spoken of sleep before in the sense of spiritual slumber
(5:6); now he applied the same image to the idea of death. This
was a quick glance back to the earlier discussion as to what will
become of 'them that fall asleep' before the Lord's return (4:13).
To be awake is to be alive; to be asleep is to have died. But
living or dying we now rejoice in the knowledge that in virtue
of His death we shall live. The prepositions are significant: He
died *for us* that we may live *with him*. If the Resurrection is not
mentioned, it is clearly implied: 'we believe that Jesus died
and rose again' (4:14). We live *with him* because His life is ours
and death can not sever the ties of that living union. It all
shows how totally we owe salvation to Him alone. What more
indeed could those converts ask, or what more did they need,
as they looked to the future? Nothing that would really matter.
'Wherefore exhort one another, and build each other up, even
as also ye do' (5:11; cf. 4:18).

Chapter Six

Prove and Hold Fast

'Prove all things; hold fast that which is good'.
1 THESSALONIANS 5:21

IT IS common to most of the Pauline Letters to find that they move to a close with a series of short maxims, and this Epistle was no exception. They are crisp, brief, easily remembered, and lay down rules for a steady, disciplined character. 'Rejoice alway; pray without ceasing; in everything give thanks: for this is the will of God in Christ Jesus to you-ward. Quench not the Spirit; despise not prophesyings; prove all things; hold fast that which is good; abstain from every form of evil. And the God of peace himself sanctify you wholly; and may your spirit and soul and body be preserved entire, without blame at the coming of our Lord Jesus Christ' (5:16-23). It was a string of short stuccato directions, of pointed and pithy commands, crowned with the words of a noble benediction. One may trace a natural connection or a sequence of thought as the maxims unfold. Thus to rejoice, pray, and give thanks are linked with the declaration about the will of God. Quench not, despise not, were commands which had to do with the Spirit or with the gifts of the Spirit. To prove and to hold fast sprang out of that context; to abstain from evil summed up the whole exhortation. Paul was writing to a church of recent converts from paganism and idolatry; he was writing as one who had apostolic authority to those who had little experience. He was deeply concerned to guide them in matters of faith and of conduct, and this exhortation was meant for the whole church, for people and elders alike. They would be quick to see how one particular saying stood out with its universal application:

36

they were to prove all things and to hold fast that which was good. That text enshrines the great Reformation doctrine of the Right of Private Judgment.

The first part of this charge urged them to make full trial of what was true: *prove all things*. This no doubt grows out of what had been said about prophesyings, a word that stood for the passionate utterance of the deep things of God. The prophets ranked second only to apostles in importance (cf. 1 Cor. 12:28; Eph. 4:11), and their function was to declare the Word of God as they were taught by the Spirit (cf. 1 Cor. 12:10). But there were false prophets as well; their words were so smooth that they would deceive even God's own elect. Therefore, although they were not to despise prophesyings, they were at the same time to prove all things. The word *prove* is derived from the assaying or testing of metals, and the meaning in this context is to put all things to the test; *all things* whatsoever, not all prophesyings only; spiritual tests were to be applied to all that claimed to be from God. Paul would have them know that it was their right to judge these things by a proper spiritual criterion, and it was their duty to do this for themselves. This would require them to compare man's words with what God has revealed in the Scriptures, and this would be imperative if they were not to be deceived by false teaching. He did not tell them to believe all that itinerant preachers might have to say; he told them to prove all things by the Word of God. That is a law which now applies to such things as doctrines, sermons, books and writings. They are to be measured with the foot-rule of the Scriptures; compared with that standard. They are to be weighed on the scales of the Bible; tested in that balance. What the Bible condemns, no matter who affirms it, we are to reject and refuse; what the Bible affirms, no matter who denies it, we are to believe and obey. 'To the law and to the testimony; if they speak not according to this word, it is because there is no light in them' (Isa. 8:20 A.V.).

The Right of Private Judgment is not meant to create division or to promote presumption, but it is the duty of all men to try to discern what is true and reject what is false or erroneous.

Christian history has seen a great variety of false teaching both within and without the Church, from the age of Gnosticism right down to the current pseudo-theology of the Rationalist. The publication of *Honest to God* by the Bishop of Woolwich in 1963 had an immediate appeal for those who lean in a Humanist direction. *The Myth of God Incarnate*, a Symposium published by a group of University Dons and Professors in 1977, was a total contradiction of the basic doctrines of the faith which most of the authors were ordained to teach and preach. Books like these have a strong fascination for those who want to rule out all that is supernatural or who only think in terms of what is intellectual. That is why the committed believer is called upon to be ready to give a reason for the hope that is in him. God has given us the promise of His Spirit and the touchstone of the Bible so that we are without excuse if we confuse truth and error. It was on this basis that Paul made his appeal to the Church at Corinth: 'I speak as to wise men; judge ye what I say' (1 Cor. 10:15). It was with this in mind that John urged his readers to act: 'Believe not every spirit, but prove the spirits, whether they are of God: because many false prophets are gone out into the world' (1 John 4:1). The people of Beroea were the noble-minded men and women who heard Paul preach and then searched the Scriptures to see 'whether these things were so' (Acts 17:11). We should follow others only so far as they follow the Lord of Truth.

The next part of this charge urged them to take firm hold of what was true: *hold fast that which is good*. This is in one sense a general expression, but it could have been used of coins whose ring was true. In this context, it meant that they were to sort out what was counterfeit and to hold fast what was authentic. The verb *to hold fast* was used twice in the Letter to the Hebrews with a special application to hope: 'Let us hold fast the confession of our hope that it waver not' (Heb. 10:23, cf. 3:6). Perhaps Paul's words anticipate the strong warning he would issue in his second Letter: they were not to allow themselves to be agitated 'either by spirit, or by word, or by epistle as from us' (2 Thess. 2:2). It would seem that there were some who claimed a kind of spirit-insight, or a verbal message, or a fraudulent epistle from him to the effect that 'the day of the Lord is now present' (2 Thess. 2:2). It was indeed urgent that they should sift what was genuine from all that was spurious and that they should hold fast that which was good. They were to grasp the truth and never let it slip from their fingers. This means in our case that we must equip ourselves with a thorough knowledge of the Bible; this is imperative if we are to become effective guardians of truth. No praise is due to the hearer who finds fault with sermons but who never reads the Bible; he must know the Bible well if he would pronounce on what is good. But it will not do to master theories in our minds if our lives do not carry equal conviction. The light of truth must shine through our minds and down to our hearts, for faith will hang on a broken reed if it does not hang on the Word of God. Therefore in great issues of truth, and where eternal verities are the stake at issue, we must rely on what God has revealed in the Bible and dare to hold it fast.

Paul knew how apt such an exhortation was in view of human failings, for he knew how easily love cools, and zeal fails, and faith flags. Jesus Himself had warned the Twelve to 'take heed and beware of the leaven of the Pharisees and Sadducees' (Matt. 16:6). The Pharisees were those who sought to add to the Law the traditions of men: they had 'made void the word of God because of (their) tradition' (Matt. 15:6). The Sadducees were those who took from the Scriptures all that was supernatural: they denied the reality of angels and argued that there was no resurrection (Matt. 22:23). Moses had warned Israel that no man should tamper with the Law as it was written: 'Ye shall not add unto the word which I command you, neither shall ye diminish from it' (Deut. 4:2; 12:32). This would find an echo in the closing words of the Bible: 'I testify unto every man that heareth the words of the prophecy of this book, If any man shall add unto them, God shall add unto him the plagues which are written in this book: and if any man shall take away from the words of the book of this prophecy, God shall take away his part from the tree of life' (Rev. 22:18-

19). Men with any understanding of the times can not fail to see how the leaven of the Pharisees and the Sadducees is still at work. The mantle of the Pharisees has fallen on those who want to add to what is written and would have us believe more than the Bible reveals. The mantle of the Sadducees has fallen on those who want to take from what is written and would have us believe less than the Bible demands. It is hard to say which holds more danger as a threat to the truth, but there are undoubtedly times when it is better to stand alone than to err with the crowd. 'Hold fast that which thou hast, that no one take thy crown' (Rev. 3:11).

It may be true that the Right of Private Judgment has sometimes been abused; but the dangers of abuse are not so grave as the dangers of neglect. The Church is not infallible; it has no guarantee of immunity from error. Let the Church of any age in any land depart from the Bible, and it will err. There was a time when the Churches of East and West had bowed their knee to the Arian heresy. There was a time when the mediaeval Church in Europe succumbed to superstition and error. General Councils were limited in authority because they were no more infallible than the Churches which they represented: 'They may err, and sometimes have erred, even in things pertaining unto God.'[1] Any one Church may err; the candle will then be removed from the candlestick. Where is the Church of Corinth or Sardis? Where is the Church of Hippo or Carthage? They erred and sank into oblivion; they have gone, and not a vestige is left. Even the best of men and ministers are fallible; they may be very dogmatic, and yet may be far from orthodox. We need grace to perceive what is crucial in the doctrines of God's great self-revelation in the Bible so that we may adhere to them with an unyielding conviction. It was in this sense that Luther singled out the doctrine of Justification by Faith Only as the article of a standing or falling church.[2] It was also in this sense that John Frith held that although there are many doctrines taught in Scripture, it is not

---

[1] Article XXI (The 39 Articles of Religion).
[2] Schmalkald Articles II. i.

necessary to hold them all as essential to salvation.[3] Paul's words ought to ring in our ears to-day: 'Prove all things: hold fast that which is good'. We are appointed guardians of the treasures of grace and truth revealed in the Bible, and we would be ungrateful sons of a noble heritage if we were to disown or ignore the Right of Private Judgment.

[3] The *Works of The Excellent Martyr of Christ, John Frith and* The *Works of Doctor Barnes*, edited by John Foxe (1573), p. 172.

Chapter Seven

Patience and Persecution

'To the end that ye may be counted worthy of the
kingdom of God, for which ye also suffer'.

2 THESSALONIANS 1:1-7

IT IS not clear who was available to take Paul's first Letter back to
the church in Thessalonica; meanwhile he and Silas and Timothy
continued to exercise their ministry in Corinth. It was not long
before fresh news reached them about that brave little band of
converts. One of their own number must have travelled down to
Corinth either with a written reply to his Letter or a verbal report
on their affairs. Paul was saddened to learn that they were now
subject to an aggravated form of persecution; but he also rejoiced
to know that the church had measured up to that trial with
patience and courage. He spoke of 'them that know not God,
and . . . them that obey not the gospel of our Lord Jesus Christ'
(1:8); this may be an indication that both Gentiles and Jews had
been active in this wave of persecution. Perhaps as in other cities
the Jews were the instigators and had stirred the Gentiles into
bitter opposition. Paul had written about all this before and was
enormously thankful that they had found grace to endure. But
his earlier Epistle had not achieved all that he had desired. He
was told of other matters which filled him with concern. These
had to do with the Second Coming of Christ: his teaching, both
oral and written, was misunderstood. These new converts had
come to think that this event was so imminent that they had lost
their grip on reality. The vague longing for His Return had
turned into dogmatic certainty that it was now at hand. This had
induced a mixed state of perilous excitement, mental ferment,
idleness, disorder. Therefore within a few weeks of his first Letter,

42

not more than six months at most, Paul found himself obliged to write again in order to correct, to instruct and to exhort.

Paul's name stands at the head of this Letter in the style of the age, but he coupled with it the names of Silas and Timothy as in the earlier Epistle: 'Paul, and Silvanus, and Timothy, unto the church of the Thessalonians in God our Father and the Lord Jesus Christ; grace to you and peace from God the Father and the Lord Jesus Christ' (1:1-2). This is identical with the salutation in the former Letter except for a minor variation in both clauses. Thus he spoke of 'God *our* Father' where the earlier Epistle spoke of 'God *the* Father'; and he caught up the phrase about 'God our Father and the Lord Jesus Christ' in order to ascribe grace and peace to 'God the Father and the Lord Jesus Christ'. These two Letters were addressed to *the church* (cf. 1 Cor. 1:2; 2 Cor. 1:1; Gal. 1:2); four others were addressed to *the saints* (Rom. 1:7; Eph. 1:1; Phil. 1:1; Col. 1:2); the remaining four Epistles were personal in character and were addressed to the recipient by name. He spoke of the church as being *in God*, having been brought into union with Him, hidden in Him as the source of every blessing. He spoke of God as *our Father*, the true Father of all them that believe, Jew and Gentile alike; and he spoke of *Jesus* as the Lord Christ whose Deity and Dominion must be seen as unique. It was in the Name of God the Father and the Lord Christ that he wished them both grace and peace. This became the standard form of greeting in all his Epistles, and the ideas behind the words recall many lovely sayings in the Psalms of David: 'The Lord is gracious; His mercy is everlasting: and His truth endureth from generation to generation' (Ps. 100:5 P.B.V.). Bishop Lightfoot's comment was that grace is the source of all real blessings; peace their end and issue.[1]

Paul went on at once to pour out his thanks to God for these converts in the language of vehemence and emotion: 'We are bound to give thanks to God alway for you, brethren, even as it is meet, for that your faith groweth exceedingly, and the love of each one of you all toward one another aboundeth' (1:3). Nothing could have been more like him in thought, feeling and expres-

[1] J. B. Lightfoot, *ibid.* p. 8.

sion. Clause followed clause without a break until he reached the
end of the tenth verse. It all flowed from the heart of that stern
but gentle servant of God and it reveals as much about him as
about those to whom he was writing. His thoughts rose far above
the level of ordinary tributes and was transformed into a hymn of
praise for all that God had wrought. He was deeply thankful for
God's grace in their lives, and he strengthened all that he had
said in his first Letter (cf. 1 Thess. 1:2-5). The first phrase lays
decided emphasis on the duty aspect of this generous utterance:
'We ought always to thank God for you' (N.I.V.). But the drive of
duty is then softened by the personal expression: 'even as it is
meet'. There is little doubt that this clause must be taken as in
parenthesis and in explanation of his sense of duty. He was *bound*
to give thanks; but he would have them know that this was
altogether *meet*, right or appropriate. And the reason why he was
bound to give thanks was because their faith was still on the
increase and their love was beyond question. Their faith was like
'a tree planted by the streams of water' (Ps. 1:3); it grew in shape
and strength *exceedingly*, fruitful and flourishing in all respects.
Their love was love for each other; it was like a river, overflowing
all its banks and spreading across the land. Such faith and such
love were glorious elements in that humble congregation.

The full measure of a thankful heart was made clear in the way
that he expressed his own response to the report of their spiritual
maturity: 'So that we ourselves glory in you in the churches of
God for your patience and faith in all your persecutions and in the
afflictions which ye endure' (1:4). His prayer for them had been
that they would 'increase and abound in love one toward another,
and toward all men' (1 Thess. 3:12). That prayer had been richly
answered, with the result that it had now become the talk of all
the churches; Paul's use of this emphatic expression shows that he
was speaking of what was out of the ordinary. It was not his habit
to boast of his converts among other churches; he was always
backward in this respect lest his words should seem like self-
praise. But the change which God had wrought in their lives was
so remarkable that he could not repress his joy. It led him to *glory*
in them; to *exult* in telling others of God's grace in their lives.

This was why they had become so well known *in the churches of God*; but which *churches* did this phrase have in view? Perhaps he had in mind 'the church of God which is at Corinth, with all the saints which are in the whole of Achaia' (2 Cor. 1:1): he may have thought of more distant churches as well (cf. 1 Thess. 1:8). At all events, the grace of God was a self-evident reality, made known to all through their *patience and faith* in the midst of persecution. The word *patience* replaced the word *love* in this fresh couplet with *faith* (cf. 1:3); it was the more appropriate virtue in a context which would focus on the continuing pressure of persecution and opposition. Paul knew only too well from long experience what this entailed, and he gloried in the patience, and endurance, and perseverance which their faith had inspired.

Paul went on to argue that they should look for signs of God's intervention since God's moral order is not destroyed by man's wicked conduct: 'which is a manifest token of the righteous judgment of God; to the end that ye may be counted worthy of the kingdom of God for which ye also suffer' (1:5). This verse as a whole, as well as the word translated *manifest token*, may be compared with a similar expression in another Epistle: 'And in nothing affrighted by the adversaries: which is for them an *evident token* of perdition, but of your salvation, and that from God' (Phil. 1:28). The real antecedent of that *token* was their *patience and faith* in the fire of persecution (1:4): their fortitude in suffering was the manifest evidence or proof of God's *righteous judgment*. Those who suffered persecution must have felt at times as though there were no justice in the affairs of men at all; but God would yet arise to visit both persecutor and persecuted with *righteous judgment*. Meanwhile God would use that time of trial to train His people in discipline and character. Judgment would come at length; but when it came, it would prove them *worthy* of His kingdom. This must recall how the Twelve had measured up to the threat of violence and suffering; they had rejoiced because 'they were *counted worthy* to suffer dishonour for the Name' (Acts 5:41). It was in this sense that Paul could tell the sister church in Philippi: 'To you it hath been granted in the behalf of Christ, not only *to believe* on him, but also *to suffer* in his behalf' (Phil. 1:29).

It was indeed for God's kingdom that these Gentile converts were compelled to suffer: not in order to gain a place in that kingdom, but to get more glory for God. And the apparent injustice of things on earth would not alter God's plan for the final triumph of what was good.

This was all part of his introduction to a great word-picture of the day of judgment when the evil-doer will be condemned and God's people will be vindicated: 'If so be that it is a righteous thing with God to recompense affliction to them that afflict you, and to you that are afflicted rest with us, at the revelation of the Lord Jesus from heaven with the angels of his power' (1:6-7). The language and imagery are those of a Hebrew Apocalypse, but this passage is more remarkable for restraint and moderation than for extravagance. It was overwhelming, catastrophic, terrifying, in its total effect, but it formed the dramatic expression of a tremendous conviction. The first phrase, *if so be* was not the *if* of doubt, but of recognised certainty (cf. Rom. 8:9, 17; 1 Cor. 8:5). It marks Paul's own deliberate belief that judgment is rooted in the sovereign character of God; it is because God is *righteous* that He will come to judge the world. He will visit those who trouble His people with trouble, and He will bring relief to those who are troubled whether in Thessalonica or in Corinth or elsewhere. This will take place 'at the *revelation* of the Lord Jesus from heaven'; nor could words be clearer in their support of the claim that 'this same Jesus . . . shall so come in like manner' as when He went into heaven (Acts 1:11 A.V.). Paul used the word *revelation* in the same sense when he spoke of 'waiting for the *revelation* of our Lord Jesus Christ' (1 Cor. 1:7). Nor will He come alone, for the mighty angels will make up His escort; it will be a day of fiery vengeance for the wicked and of endless glory for His people (cf. 1:8-10). When that day comes and He returns, let the sinner tremble and let the saint rejoice!

Chapter Eight

The Mystery of Lawlessness

'Remember ye not that when I was yet with you, I told you these things?'

2 THESSALONIANS 2:1-7.

PAUL NOW turned to the main purpose which had prompted him to write this Letter. He had referred to 'the revelation of the Lord Jesus from heaven' (1:7); but he knew that there was a good deal of erroneous speculation about this great event. He had indeed spoken to them about these things while he was yet with them (cf. 2:5). But there was so much that they had misunderstood: they seemed to think that the end of the world would come upon them at any moment. This had given rise to a state of mind in which sensation, excitement, confusion, were all dangerously mingled, and he had to address himself to this situation in order to prevent the growth of near hysteria. He employed the language of personal entreaty as he had done before: 'Now we beseech you, brethren, touching the coming of our Lord Jesus Christ and our gathering together unto him' (2:1). *We beseech you*: so he wrote, as he had written before (cf. 1 Thess. 4:1; 5:12). This had been phrased still more strongly in the first case: 'We beseech and exhort you in the Lord Jesus' (1 Thess. 4:1). It was calculated to arrest their notice and evoke a response. The word *touching* might be better rendered *concerning* and points to the subjects about which he proposed to speak: these were the return of Christ in glory and our glorious reunion with Him. These two themes had dominated the great passage in his former Letter: 'The Lord himself shall descend from heaven, with a shout, with the voice of the archangel, and with the trump of God: and the dead in Christ shall rise first: then we that are alive . . . shall with them

47

be caught up in the clouds to meet the Lord in the air: and so shall we ever be with the Lord' (1 Thess. 4:16-17).

These twin aspects of the Second Coming dwarf all other details, and it was with this in mind that he set out to entreat them to listen: 'To the end that ye be not quickly shaken from your mind, nor yet be troubled, either by spirit, or by word, or by epistle as from us, as that the day of the Lord is now present' (2:2). He was deeply concerned because these new converts had been rudely *shaken* in their mental outlook; they were *troubled* or *alarmed* (N.I.V.) by things which they had heard and which seemed to possess solid authority. They were disturbed, and he would put them on their guard not to allow their own better judgment to be easily overthrown. Paul did not seem to know what had happened to precipitate this crisis; what was clear was that his name was being used to support the false rumours and wrong ideas which had been spread around. Did these rumour-mongers claim his authority on the ground of some fresh spiritual revelation they had received? Was there something he was alleged to have said which seemed to favour their claims? Did they pretend that they had a letter in which he was supposed to have lent his support to such speculations? Something had been circulated as though it came *from us*; it was disconcerting that he could not be sure whether it was supposed to be the result of spirit-insight, or of oral report, or of a forged letter. It was as though he were trying to see clearly something that was hidden in the shadows; there was nothing he could do to make it emerge into the light. But the rumours were all to the effect that *the Day of the Lord* was just at hand. This was not true, and he vehemently denied that any such report had come from him.

So they were not to be deceived, not by anyone nor by anything: 'Let no man beguile you in any wise: for it will not be, except the falling away come first, and the man of sin be revealed, the son of perdition' (2:3). They were not to be led astray, whether by the means he had just mentioned, or in any other manner. He went on at once to furnish reasons for this warning, and they are as striking as any utterance in either Epistle. The phrase *it will not be* is in italics and the grammar is so broken that *the Day of the*

Lord must be understood: 'for *that day* will not come' before a great apostasy occurs (N.I.V.). The literature of Apocalypse foretold such an event in awful and highly figurative language; it was endorsed by the Son of Man as well as by Paul himself (cf. Matt. 24:4-12; 1 Tim. 4:1-3; 2 Tim. 3:1-9). This apostasy or *falling away* in the last days must point to a massive array of all Satan's forces in a final revolt. Lightfoot notes that the word itself implies that the opposition must spring up from within rather than from without; it must arise either from Jews or from apostate Christians who could be said to have fallen away from God; but it does not refer to the Gentiles, and this excludes many conjectural notions about *the man of sin*.[1] It is not clear from the grammar whether this revelation is the climax of the *falling away* or whether it is identical with the apostasy. History has been plentiful in its record of 'many antichrists' (1 John 2:18); but 'the man of lawlessness' (R.V.M.), 'the son of perdition' (John 17:12), will be the last and most infamous antichrist of all. He will be made known when the end is near; he is doomed to ultimate destruction.

Paul's grim concept of the man of sin may have been based on Antiochus Epiphanes, but his symbolism moves beyond the horizons of history to a final cosmic conflict: 'He that opposeth and exalteth himself against all that is called God or that is worshipped; so that he sitteth in the temple of God, setting himself forth as God' (2:4). This language is reminiscent of prophecies in Daniel (cf. Dan. 7:25; 8:9-12); of one prophecy in particular: 'He shall exalt himself, and magnify himself above every god, and shall speak marvellous things against the God of gods' (Dan. 11:36). It is applied by Paul to a person who will at last head up all the forces of evil and apostasy. Paul had known in himself what the temptation was like to be *exalted above measure* (2 Cor. 12:7 A.V.), but had been held in check by a thorn in the flesh. But the man of sin would know no restraint; he was the great adversary who would *exalt himself* as though he were equal with God. The phrase *all that is called God* is so wide that it includes the false gods of heathen mythology as well as the one

[1] J. B. Lightfoot, *ibid.* p. 111.

true God of Israel; and the phrase *all . . . that is worshipped* includes all 'objects of worship', both persons and idols (cf. Acts 17:23). The end result of that false self-exaltation will be made clear when he invades God's own sanctuary in order to proclaim himself as God. Lightfoot points out that this figure could have emerged from 'the insane attempt' of the Emperor Caius to erect his statue in the temple.[2] Jesus Himself had warned the Twelve that 'the abomination of desolation' would stand where it ought not (Mark 13:14). So the resurgence of evil will culminate in an attempt to drive God from His throne. There are always men who would like to lead God to the edge of the universe and bow Him out; but this act of usurpation will be the ultimate blasphemy.

But such vivid apocalyptic language ought not to have been a surprise; it was only supplementing what he had told them while he was there in person: 'Remember ye not, that when I was yet with you, I told you these things?' (2:5). Such a call to *remember* was not uncommon nor in the least improbable. We can not tell what the style or detail of his preaching had been; the one slight hint is that he had spoken of 'another king, one Jesus' (Acts 17:7). This had formed the pretext for the accusation that his preaching had been hostile to the decrees of the Roman Caesar. Perhaps the fact that the Emperor had been deified would not only not escape his notice, but would account for his easily remembered emphasis on the kingship of Jesus. We can only fill out what must have been the real substance of his oral teaching by a careful study of the text of these two Letters. But he assumed that they could call to mind what he had said as though it were but yesterday. It was all clear to them because of their active recollection; it is by no means clear to us because of our lack of background information. As a result, this passage as a whole is one of the most obscure and difficult paragraphs in Paul's writings. He sent their thoughts back to the time while he was yet with them when he had been wont to tell them these things. The use of the imperfect tense shows that this had been more than a casual reference. 'I used to tell you' (N.I.V.); I often spoke of these things: they had been at the heart of his preaching. But Old

---

[2] J. B. Lightfoot, *ibid.* p. 113.

Testament allusions in an apocalyptic framework may well have been misunderstood: they were Gentile converts, with Greek culture and under the domination of Rome.

This brief parenthesis gave way to a deliberate appeal to facts that were within their own knowledge: 'And now ye know that which restraineth, to the end that he may be revealed in his season. For the mystery of lawlessness doth already work: only there is one that restraineth now, until he be taken out of the way' (2:6-7). *Ye know*: they knew what now we do not know; that was the factor of restraint. But Paul did not elaborate that veiled remark; it was enough for his purpose to say that the man of sin had not yet appeared because of some restraining influence. What was it? Was it the Roman Empire? Was it the Emperor Claudius? Or was it something totally different? While that restraint remained, the man of sin would not emerge; but it would be removed at length so that the man of sin would stand revealed at his destined moment. Just as the Son of God would be *revealed* at His coming (cf. 1:7), so would the man of sin be *revealed* in the fulness of time; meanwhile his presence was hidden although his activities were potent as a force in the world. The whole picture would be heightened by the bold phrase about *the mystery of lawlessness*. It is in strong contrast with his use of a like phrase on another occasion: *the mystery of godliness*. (1 Tim. 3:16). We know what that was: it was 'God, manifest in the flesh'. The mystery of godliness was the incarnation of God in the Person of the Christ-Child. The mystery of lawlessness was the incarnation of all that is evil in the man of sin. That last terrible mystery is the ultimate counterfeit of Christ Himself, and it must be fully revealed before *the Day of the Lord* comes (cf. 2:2). Meanwhile it can only work in secret because of that restraining influence; the time for that to be *taken out of the way* is in the hand of God.

Chapter Nine

Good Hope Through Grace

'But the Lord is faithful who shall stablish you and guard
you from the evil one'.

2 THESSALONIANS 3:1-5

THESE TWO Letters both fall into two parts, and their structure
provides quite an instructive parallel. The first part in each
case is largely taken up with explanation and concludes with a
splendid benediction (1 Thess. 3:11-13; 2 Thess. 2:16-17);
and the second part in each case begins in the same way and
ends with a further benediction (1 Thess. 5:23; 2 Thess. 3:16).
The first section of this second Letter comes to a close on a note
which one might have thought would leave nothing further to
add: 'Now our Lord Jesus Christ Himself, and God our Father
which loved us and gave us eternal comfort and good hope
through grace, comfort your hearts and stablish them in every
good work and word' (2 Thess. 2:16-17). These words must
rank among the most lovely of all Paul's prayers for his
converts. It is significant that he spoke of *our Lord Jesus Christ*
before he mentioned *God our Father*; the order is identical with
that in the words of the grace (cf. 2 Cor. 13:13). Paul did this
in a way that would equate the Son with the Father as the
Author of the blessing which he meant to pronounce. But the
reference to the Father is then amplified by the clauses in which
the words *loved* and *gave* are predominant. They were in fact
aorist participles, for that divine love was manifested in the
highest degree when the Father gave us His Son (cf. John 3:16).
That love and that gift are the source of our 'everlasting
consolation and good hope through grace' (A.V.); that is, never-
failing strength and comfort in all present circumstances; calm

certainty and confidence in all future expectations; and all as an act of grace on the part of God. Such hope would shed its light on their path so as to strenghten and stablish their hearts in all things both great and small; not in *works* only, but in *words* also; so that their lives would reflect His glory.

Paul then turned to a new section in order to correct certain problems in their conduct of which he had been told: 'Finally, brethren, pray for us, that the word of the Lord may run and be glorified, even as also it is with you' (3:1). The word *finally* introduced what he proposed to say (cf. 1 Thess. 4:1), but he began on a note of personal interest. He had dealt with the main issues which had prompted him to write this Letter, but there were still some things of weight to bring forward. And first he would urge them to *pray*. This verb is a present imperative and is in an emphatic position. They were to pray *for us*; for Silas and Timothy as well as for him. They were to hold fast his teaching (cf. 2:15), and to keep on praying. He poured out his own heart in prayer for his converts; he was always just as eager that they should give themselves to prayer on his behalf. This was not a selfish request; he longed for God's Word as spoken by His servants to speed on its way in Corinth. *The Word of the Lord* was a phrase which he had used before (1 Thess. 1:8), and it must mean *the Word* given by God. The verb *may run* is a possible allusion to a verse in the Psalms: 'His word runneth very swiftly' (Ps. 147:15). It may also reflect the Greek games in Corinth and Paul's favourite metaphor from the foot-race. At all events, he would have it *run* in order to achieve its purpose; that is, that it might be received with honour, or *glorified* by its effect on the hearers. The last clause has curious overtones of human pathos and wistful longing: *even as also it is with you*. Did he survey the harsh realities of life in that ultra-pagan city of Corinth? Did that make him recall with a redoubled sense of nostalgia the effect of his preaching in Thessalonica?

But there was a second aspect of this situation about which he would have them pray: 'And that we may be delivered from unreasonable and evil men; for all have not faith' (3:2). He knew only too well from long experience the obstacles that surrounded his work. His troubles in Corinth were a match for theirs in Thessalonica. He felt a strong need for constant deliverance from such determined enmity. It would have been less than human if he had not sought by every legitimate means to ensure his own safety. It would be in the same spirit that he enjoined on the Church at Rome the urgent duty of prayer: 'Now I beseech you, brethren, by our Lord Jesus Christ and by the love of the Spirit, that ye strive together with me in your prayers to God for me, that I may be delivered from them that are disobedient in Judaea' (Rom. 15:30-31). The Jews; always the Jews, or so it seemed, for he had in mind a special local group in Corinth as in Jerusalem rather than the threat of adversaries at large. The Jews had not only opposed him, but blasphemed as well, and he had been provoked into one of his most drastic retorts: 'Your blood be upon your own heads; I am clean: from henceforth I will go unto the Gentiles' (Acts 17:6). They were *wicked and evil men* (N.I.V.), active in the instigation of what was wrong, ready to lend themselves to a deliberate campaign to oppose and destroy. This would be most clearly seen when in due course they dragged Paul before the new Pro-consul Gallio in order to arraign him on the false charge of acting against the law. That must have been in the future when he wrote this Letter, but their prayers would not be in vain. The last sentence was in parenthesis; they knew that not all men had faith. The fact that the definite article precedes the word *faith* shows that what he had in view was the Gospel; only the few possessed that body of teaching as their portion.

Paul turned from man's faithless outlook to the absolute faithfulness of God: 'But the Lord is faithful, who shall stablish you and guard you from the evil one' (3:3). There is the same play on the same words and ideas in a similar utterance, though it is in the form of a rhetorical question rather than a direct statement: 'For what if some were without faith? shall their want of faith make of none effect the faithfulness of God?' (Rom. 3:3). There is no doubt that the faithfulness of God was a favourite theme throughout his apostolic career (cf. 1 Cor. 1:9; 2 Tim. 2:13). This verse reads just like an echo of the closing words in his first Letter: 'Faithful is he that calleth you, who will also do it' (1 Thess. 5:24). He was ready to ground his strong sense of assurance in the character of God; he dared to claim that it is God Himself who stands behind all His people in need or trial. This God would make them both strong and stable; He would plant their feet on a rock from which they would never be moved; He would *stablish* or *strengthen* them against all their adversaries (cf. N.I.V.). Paul had turned from himself to his converts, from his own anxieties in Corinth to their problems in Thessalonica, and he had done this so naturally that the transition could almost pass unnoticed. This is one more illustration of the way in which he identified himself with his readers, and the sense of identity is still further strengthened by the way in which he carried on the same line of thought. The God who is faithful would guard them from *the Evil One*; whether from Satan, or Satan's agent. If *the Evil One* were Satan, he would be seen as the father of the *evil men* whose assaults had been instigated by him (cf. 3:2).[1] And if it were the man of sin, however frightening that might be, the Lord would overcome.

So Paul did not hesitate to declare his confidence on their account: 'And we have confidence in the Lord touching you, that ye both do and will do the things which we command' (3:4). This verse seems to follow from the original request that they should pray for him (cf. 3:1); it would express the confidence and certainty with which he looked to them. His trust was *in the Lord* in so far as they were concerned; it was removed from all merely human calculation because it was rooted in Him. The God who is faithful will do all that He has promised and Paul had no hesitation in grounding his expectations upon this fact: 'Being confident of this very thing, that he which began a good work in you will perfect it until the day of Jesus Christ' (Phil. 1:6). Therefore he was bold to say that he could rely on them to do as he had asked. But he broadened

[1] cf. J. B. Lightfoot, *ibid.* p. 127.

the whole concept with an application to all *the things which we command*. When he had asked for prayer, it had been more in the nature of a request than a command; but there had been commands. They were to let no man deceive them with plausible argument (2:3); they were to hold fast the primary traditions which they had learned from him (2:15). They had listened to his teaching in times gone by; so now they would listen to his commands for the future. This expression of confidence was his style of approach, with tact and skill, to a whole new series of directions, some of which would be hard to voice, harder still to obey. The series would begin with words that would brook no nonsense: 'Now we *command* you, brethren, in the name of our Lord Jesus Christ, that ye withdraw yourselves from every brother that walketh disorderly' (3:7). But his soft and gentle approach would have inclined them to assent even before they knew what was required.

But before he embarked on those commands, his confidence found utterance in prayer: 'And the Lord direct your hearts into the love of God and into the patience of Christ' (3:5). This was so like him in tone and spirit that it helps to explain why he could rely on them to respond. He had declared his trust in them; therefore let the Lord be their guide. *The Lord*, even Jesus, to whom this Name applies throughout the whole section: He would *direct* their hearts into the love of God and the patience of Christ. He had used the same word in the former Letter: 'Now may our God and Father Himself, and our Lord Jesus, *direct* our way unto you' (1 Thess. 3:11). That had meant to make a straight path by the removal of all obstacles. But in this case it had a more figurative application and its meaning was to open a way in the inmost region of their spirit. This would allow them to focus their whole being on the love and patience which were in view; it was indeed as though he would draw their inmost spirit into the light of God's presence. He had spoken before of their 'labour of love and patience of hope in our Lord Jesus Christ' (1 Thess. 1:3); but these words go further as a prayer that their whole experience of that love and patience might be deepened. *The love of God* might speak of God's love for them or their love for God; it might be a comprehensive phrase which would take in both ideas. *Patience* refers to a steadfast will to endure, and *the patience of Christ* means that it was exemplified in Him. John the Divine was to share in 'the tribulation and kingdom and *patience* which are in Jesus' (Rev. 1:9). If Paul's readers were only to enter into that love and that patience, they would gladly respond to his commands.

Chapter Ten

Fellowship in the Gospel

'I have you in my heart'.

PHILIPPIANS 1:1-8.

THE COLONY of Philippi had been founded about one hundred miles beyond Thessalonica beside the great Roman highway called the Via Egnatia. It had been the scene of Paul's first missionary labours on arrival in Macedonia and its converts were the first-fruits of his witness on the European mainland. There was more than ordinary depth and fulness in the affinities that bound his heart to them; he could scarcely write to them without a flood of nostalgic memory: 'Paul and Timothy, servants of Christ Jesus, to all the saints in Christ Jesus which are at Philippi, with the bishops and deacons: grace to you and peace from God our Father and the Lord Jesus Christ' (1:1-2). It was on a sabbath by the river, in a place where prayer was wont to be made, that he had found Lydia, a purple-seller from Thyatira, 'whose heart the Lord opened' (Acts 16:14). It was out in the street that he had cast out the unclean spirit which had driven a poor girl to follow them with her cry: 'These men are servants of the Most High God which proclaim unto you the way of salvation, (Acts 16:17). It was there that he and Silas had been scourged by Roman lictors, placed in stocks and shut up in the inmost prison. It was there that the doors of the prison were thrown open by a midnight earthquake and that the jailer cast himself at their feet with the cry: 'Sirs, what must I do to be saved?' (Acts 16:30). The next day, they left the Colony at the request of the magistrates. But Paul was not driven away: he had left with honour and for the sake of peace. But no church was ever dearer to him than his converts in

Philippi and they grew in number with the passage of time. Therefore when he came to write this Letter, perhaps from Ephesus, perhaps from Rome, he could address them all in a single comprehensive phrase of gentle beauty: 'all the saints in Christ Jesus which are at Philippi'.

Paul's love and care for his converts were never more tenderly expressed than in this Letter; it was as though memory overflowed and poured itself out with pure joy: 'I thank my God upon all my remembrance of you, always in every supplication of mine on behalf of you all making my supplication with joy, for your fellowship in furtherance of the gospel from the first day until now' (1:3-5). He could not call them to mind without renewing his thanks to God, and this led him into a brief aside. Remembrance and thankfulness sought expression in prayer, and this was the spontaneous prayer of one who could not refrain. He could not think of his converts without praying for them, and he could not name them in prayer except with joy. He gave thanks to God and poured out his heart in prayer on their behalf. But this parenthesis did not disturb his train of thought and he went on to thank God as he remembered their *fellowship in furtherance of the Gospel*.

This reference to *fellowship* ought not to be isolated from his use of the same word in other contexts (2:1; 3:10). It was rich in meaning and set out an ideal relationship. There is little doubt that in this passage it was meant to apply to the love and good-will which had prompted their giving and support on his behalf. It was enough to hint at this for the moment; there would be more to say before he had finished. But their generous interest had been with a view to the spread of the Gospel, and it had been sustained *from the first day until now*. It had been like this 'in the beginning of the Gospel' (4:15) when Lydia had constrained him to become her guest (Acts 16:15); it was like this now when Epaphroditus had come to minister to him in prison (4:18). There had never been any breach in that generous fellowship, and it was a reciprocal experience.

The memory of fellowship which had continued from the beginning even *until now* was enough to prompt another reflection: 'Being confident of this very thing, that he which began a good work in you will perfect it until the day of Jesus Christ' (1:6). The grace of God already manifest in their lives led him to speak of the yet unknown future with a sense of absolute confidence. This expression of confidence was in fact firmly rooted in one great basic experience: *this very thing*. What did he mean? It could only refer to the crisis of their initial conversion; that was the work of all works which God had begun in them. Paul would often recall his own conversion on the road to Damascus, and in the same spirit he would often refer to the time when God's grace had first taken its hold on his converts. He was unshakably convinced that that work of grace would receive its crown when the day that brings the return of Christ shall dawn. God will *perfect* the work which He began; He will perform all that He has promised. His sovereign initiative is seen in the primary work of conversion; His absolute faithfulness is seen in His perseverance with His saints right on to the end. This was the thought of the Psalmist in an hour of troubled adversity: 'I will cry unto God Most High; unto God that performeth all things for me' (Ps. 57:2). This confidence finds expression in still clearer terms in another Psalm of thanksgiving: 'The Lord will perfect that which concerneth me' (Ps. 138:8). It was in line with Paul's declaration to the sister church of Thessalonica: 'Faithful is he that calleth you, who will also do it' (1 Thess. 5:24). What then if they had to contend with hardship and persecution? They were buoyed up with the knowledge that God would bring all His work to glorious fruition in that great day of Christ's return.

The next words lay bare the depth of his rich pastoral affection: 'Even as it is right for me to be thus minded on behalf of you all, because I have you in my heart' (1:7). It was as though he were to say that whatever might be right for others, it was right for him of all men to be of this mind, to think and feel like this, where they were concerned. The word *to be minded, to think* (A.V.), was a favourite expression in this Letter and it conveys the idea of sympathetic care and understanding concern (cf. 2:2, 5; 3:15, 19; 4:2, 10). A good illustration of Paul's use of this word in a context with a different emphasis may be quoted: 'Let us therefore, as many as be perfect, *be thus minded*: and if in anything ye *are otherwise minded*, even this shall God reveal unto you' (3:15). It means a great deal when we have others in mind: we think of them; we care for them; we pray for them; we plan for them. But if 'the saints . . . at Philippi' (1:1) were to ask why it was right for Paul of all men to think like this of them, he could only answer in terms of a beautiful metaphor. It was 'because I have you in my heart'; they were in the stronghold of love. He was often deeply aware of his converts, as though he were present with them even when in fact he was far away (cf. 1 Cor. 5:3; Col. 2:5). But his thought in this verse goes much further in its picture of those who were always secure in the fortress of his own heart. So too he could assure his Thessalonian converts that though he was bereft of them for a season, they were still in his heart (1 Thess. 2:17). The same thought is expressed with a wonderful tenderness in his appeal to the church at Corinth: what he said to them was not said in order to condemn; 'but simply because, as I said before, whether we live or die, you live in our hearts' (2 Cor. 7:3, J. B. Phillips).

Paul went on to explain that the real ground for that declaration of his devotion to their interests was the fact that they shared his own supreme passion: 'inasmuch as, both in my bonds and in the defence and confirmation of the gospel, ye all are partakers with me of grace' (1:7). *My bonds*: this is the first mention of his bonds and imprisonment in this Letter; he was under restraint for Christ's sake and for theirs as well. He would have more to say about it in the course of the Letter, but there was no need to enlarge on the circumstances. The church must have been well aware of his situation when it resolved to send Epaphroditus on a special visit to his prison quarters. But the mention of his *bonds* led him to speak of *the defence and confirmation* of the Gospel; that is, his work as an apologist and an evangelist in the cause of God's great good news. These words may be legal terms which describe his trial either before the imperial court or a provincial magistrate, and in this case there is a clear contrast between his bonds and the trial itself. It was as if he were to say: 'whether I am in prison or whether I am arraigned before the judge'.[1] Look at it from either standpoint, it could make no substantial difference. He had them in his heart; and they partook with him of grace. They were one with him in his bonds and in his trial; he was one with them in the grace of God. He saw his own conflict as one which was on their behalf and in which they were called to share; and he saw their experience of grace as one which they shared in common with him. Was this surprising conclusion just a glorious paradox in words only or in fact and in truth? There was no room for doubt; distance had no effect on the closeness of this fellow-feeling which was forged in the grace of God.[2]

Because there were limits to his human capacity for such love and longing, he was constrained to make it all centre in the Person of Christ Himself: 'For God is my witness, how I long after you all in the tender mercies of Christ Jesus' (1:8). Both separation and imprisonment made their contribution to this vigorous assertion of his feelings towards those dearly loved converts. It is very striking to see how he could call on God as his witness, though he only did so in a spirit of great solemnity or when he was moved to the depths of his being. There were several occasions when strong feeling constrained him to use such language. 'God is my witness', he wrote to the church at Rome, '. . . how unceasingly I make mention of you, . . . for I long to see you, that I may impart unto you some spiritual gift' (Rom. 1:9-11; cf. 2 Cor. 1:23; 1 Thess. 2:5). But there is no other passage in which the same intensity of feeling is expressed as in this verse. He dared to claim that God Himself could bear witness to the fact that he yearned for them with the very yearning of Christ Jesus. The phrase *in the tender mercies of Christ Jesus* may be taken as though it read, 'in the very heart of Jesus'. It was as though he were to say: 'You are in my heart

---

[1] cf. Ralph P. Martin: *The Epistle of Paul to the Philippians* (Tyndale Press) pp. 63–64.
[2] R. P. Martin, *ibid.* p. 63.

as you are in His heart too; I love you all and long for you in Christ and for Christ's sake alone'. It was said of David Livingstone that the word *Africa* would be found engraved on his heart; and it might have been said of the Apostle that the name *Philippi* had been stamped on his heart. It is indeed a tender and moving declaration of his inmost feelings; the bonds that bound his heart to theirs were far stronger than the chains on his wrists. That tenderness and affection run right through the Letter: 'My brethren', he wrote, 'beloved and longed for, my joy and crown' (4:1).

Chapter Eleven

The Mind of Christ

'Have this mind in you, which was also in Christ Jesus'.
PHILIPPIANS 2:1-5.

THE FIRST chapter had been enough to show that this Letter was rich in the generous overflow of a warm-hearted affection. It was almost as though there were no error to correct, no conduct to reprove, no fault to find. Nevertheless when Epaphroditus came to visit Paul in prison as a messenger from the church at Philippi, he brought news which caused a sense of disquiet. As a result, Paul's one anxiety was lest their real oneness of mind should be impaired; there is some reference to it in every chapter of this short Epistle. The first is no more than a hint: 'Only let your manner of life be worthy of the gospel of Christ: that whether I come and see you or be absent, I may hear of your state, that ye stand fast in one spirit, with one soul striving for the faith of the gospel' (1:27). The next reference is more decided: 'Fulfil ye my joy, that ye be of the same mind, having the same love, being of one accord, of one mind' (2:2). The third occasion is more indirect: 'Let us therefore, as many as be perfect, be thus minded: and if in anything ye are otherwise minded, even this shall God reveal unto you: only, whereunto we have already attained, by that same rule let us walk' (3:15-16). At last these broad hints were made plain as he named two members of the congregation who were at odds with each other: 'I exhort Euodia and I exhort Syntyche to be of the same mind in the Lord' (4:2). They were fellow workers; their names were in the book of life; but they were incompatible, and the friction between them was a threat to the health of the whole congregation. This was the one dark

cloud which he discerned on the horizon over Philippi. It was
still no bigger than a man's hand; but who could tell to what
it might yet grow? Therefore in this passage, Paul made it
clear how much he longed to see that cloud once and for all
dissolved.

Paul's first words were an exhortation to be like-minded: 'If
there is therefore any comfort in Christ, if any consolation of
love, if any fellowship of the Spirit, if any tender mercies and
compassions' (2:1). The word *therefore* points back to his
summons for them to 'stand fast in one spirit' (1:27) and it
leads on in a graceful manner to his moving exhortation. It was
a most tender appeal on the ground of all true spiritual
experience; nothing was more certain in his judgment than the
realities which he singled out for mention. The word *if* held no
trace of doubt; he was in fact so sure of those realities that
he chose such a word for the sake of uncommon emphasis. It
was as though he were to write in the spirit of conviction and
certainty: 'If you know anything of real encouragement in
Christ; if you know anything of the consolation that flows from
the love of God; if you know anything of the communion and
fellowship of the Spirit'. Then he broadened the whole appeal
to take in their experience of sympathy and compassion: 'if you
know anything of the tender mercies of God'. The thought
may be compared with that of a Petrine saying: 'If ye have
tasted that the Lord is gracious' (1 Pet. 2:3). If this were true,
as was indeed the case, then he would plead with them: listen
to me; hear my appeal; 'fulfil my joy' (2:2). When at length
Epaphroditus returned to Philippi and the congregation met to
hear that Letter read aloud, one likes to think that these words
would bring them to the tip-toe of eager desire. What would
they not do for such a one as 'Paul the aged' (Philemon 9), and
now in bonds? What would they not give to fill his cup with
joy? That most moving appeal would make them strain their
ears for the next words which would tell them how to respond.

Paul's great fourfold appeal was matched by the fourfold
response for which he asked: 'Fulfil ye my joy, that ye be of the
same mind, having the same love, being of one accord, of one

mind' (2:2). When those words were read out to the little band of converts in the church at Philippi, they may have felt strangely surprised. This was the last kind of request that would occur to them; but its meaning was quite beyond mistake. Paul had heaped phrase on phrase in this appeal for unity and amity. It was something that left no room for prejudice or jealousy or bitterness or resentment. His great desire for them was a union of heart in true family fellowship. Like-mindedness in the sense of this verse is the secret of the spiritual health and welfare of any congregation in any circumstances. This is what lay at the heart of the Lord's prayer for all who believe in Him: 'That they may be *one*, even as we are *one*; I in them, and thou in me' (John 17:22-23). This was the spirit in which the disciples were to assemble on the day of Pentecost: 'They were all with *one* accord in one place' when they were all filled with the Holy Ghost (Acts 2:1 A.V.). Were the saints at Philippi ignorant of this basic law of Christian fellowship? Were they reluctant to take necessary measures for their mutual well-being? Had they failed to recognise the threat to their essential unity in that pagan environment? They could not be indifferent to the yearning of their father in God; each phrase as it was read aloud would sound a fresh summons for them to seek a true like-mindedness as in the sight of God. It was indeed one great glory of the Gospel that it broke down tremendous barriers and swept away things that divide. There is neither east nor west, black nor white, rich nor poor; for all are *one* if they are in the Lord Jesus. (Gal. 3:28).

Paul's next words were an exhortation to be lowly-minded: 'Doing nothing through faction or through vainglory, but in lowliness of mind each counting other better than themselves' (2:3). Paul's choice of words shows up the real nature of whatever was disruptive in the life of the church. *Faction* was the word he had used before to denote the troublesome character of those who were opposed to him (1:17), while *vainglory* was the motive force that stirred men to strife. There are always subtle dangers in an arrogant or aggressive spirit, in the kind of person who is so sure that he is right that he becomes narrow, critical and dogmatic. This may be true of a young man who can be so patronising, or of an old man who can be so domineering. Perhaps Paul was unconsciously drawing on his own past experience; what was he like as a young man? He had told Herod Agrippa: 'I verily thought with myself that I ought to do many things contrary to the name of Jesus of Nazareth' (Acts 26:9). His life had been dominated by colossal self-interest for he only thought with himself (cf. Luke 18:11). There was no thought for God; it was just a soliloquy. He did what he wanted to do, and he outstripped many of his own age in what he thought was zeal for God: 'being more exceedingly zealous for the traditions of my fathers' (Gal. 1:14). But he had been humbled in the dust at the feet of Christ and he had learnt the need to be lowly-minded. It grieved him to think of party factions or petty quarrels springing up at Philippi, just as it was to grieve Cromwell when in August 1650 he wrote to the obdurate theologians in the General Assembly at Edinburgh: 'Is it therefore infallibly agreeable to the Word of God, all that *you* say? I beseech you, in the bowels of Christ, think it possible you may be mistaken'.[1]

But the grace of God will stain the pride of all our self-will, and the lowly-minded man will learn to honour others more than himself: 'Not looking each of you to his own things, but each of you also to the things of others' (2:4). This was in the very spirit of Him who was 'meek and lowly in heart' (Matt. 11:29), and who came, not to please Himself, but to care for others. To be meek and lowly-minded are both essentially Christ-like virtues; they were despised in the pagan world as signs of weakness. The two ideas are closely related, but they are not identical. Lowly-minded conduct will never give offence; meekness will never take offence. Men who are quick to give or take offence reveal their own lack of inner security; they are preoccupied with their *own things* to an extent which makes them discount *the things of others*. To be lowly-minded will teach men to walk with humility in the presence of God

---

[1] *Oliver Cromwell's Letters and Speeches*, edited by Thomas Carlyle, (five volume edition, 1871). Vol. iii. p.18.

and this will soon reveal itself in a loving concern on behalf of others. This is finely illustrated in the friendship between Henry Venn, the moderate Calvinist, and John Fletcher, the seraphic Arminian, in an age of bitter controversy. Venn described John Fletcher as 'a luminary – a luminary did I say? He was a sun! I have known all the great men for these fifty years, but I have known none like him'.[2] He was 'a man of fire, all on the stretch to do good, to lose not a day, not an hour'.[3]. Fletcher came to visit him at Huddersfield and preached to his congregation. Venn was moved to the depths of his being and went up to thank him with all his heart. To his surprise, Fletcher started back, raised his hands, and began to exclaim: 'Pardon, pardon, pardon, O my God!' Venn understood; he could not bear praise for himself when it should be ascribed to God alone.[4] That was true *lowliness of mind*.

Then Paul lifted his thoughts to the highest level of all: 'Have this mind in you, which was also in Christ Jesus' (2:5). This was the most compelling incentive he could ever propose for unity and lowliness of mind. Would they want to know a little more of the mind that was in Christ Jesus? He would tell them. Then, in incidental fashion, he brought in a long and profound statement on the Person of Christ. He did not write in the spirit of speculation or controversy; it was not his basic purpose to provide fresh insights into great questions of theology. His one object was to focus their thoughts on the Lord Christ as the divine pattern for the spirit of self-effacing fellowship. There is no verb in the Greek text for the second portion of this sentence and this is brought out in another translation: 'Have this mind among yourselves, which you have in Christ Jesus' (R.S.V.). This is strengthened by the obvious relation between the two phrases: *in you . . . in Christ Jesus*. They were to have the same mind in union with one another as they had in union with Him. What was the mind that was in Christ Jesus? It is seen here in the astonishing condescension

[2] *The Life and Times of Selina, Countess of Huntingdon*, Vol. II p. 71.
[3] *The Life and A Selection from the Letters of the Late Henry Venn* p. 376.
[4] *Ibid.* p. 582.

of the Lord from glory. He was willing to make Himself of no reputation; He took the form of a servant and came in the likeness of men. He led His life on earth in the spirit of surrender and sacrifice, and the last point to which such a life could go was to die: but it was no ordinary death He endured; it was even death on the cross (cf. 2:6-8). That was the mind which was in Christ Jesus; let that mind be in you. Would not such an appeal evoke the most tender and wistful response in Philippi? Now it is for us to lift our eyes far above that prison cell, and to hear the voice of Jesus Himself making the same appeal: 'Fulfil My joy'. Be like-minded; be lowly-minded; be Christ-minded: let this mind be in you which was also in Me.

Chapter Twelve

Toward the Goal

'I press on toward the goal unto the prize of the high
calling of God in Christ Jesus'.

PHILIPPIANS 3:12-16.

PAUL'S HIGH spiritual aspiration had soared to a noble climax
in a statement that was far more self-revealing than was his
wont: 'That I may know him, and the power of his resurrection,
and the fellowship of his sufferings, becoming conformed unto
his death, if by any means I may attain unto the resurrection
from the dead' (3:10-11). The sequence of events in the life of
the Son of Man meant of necessity that His passion took place
before He rose again. It may therefore cause some surprise to
find that Paul referred to them in the reverse order. The best
explanation is the simplest, and it is true to life. It is easy for
men to want to share in His resurrection power; it is far less
easy to wish to share in His sacrificial love. There may not be
many whom God can trust either with the one or with the
other, but this man could not be content until he had come to
know Christ in the fulness of His grace and mercy. That is why
it was not enough for him to draw on the strength of His
resurrection power; he had to go further and drink from the
cup of His sacrificial love as well. That fellowship of suffering
would be the means by which he would be made conformable
to His death and passion; and that identity with His resurrection would be the means by which he would attain to the final
resurrection. The phrase *if by any means* did not mark any lack
of personal assurance as to his share in that event. It may have
glanced at the immediate issue of his trial which was still in
the balance; that might prove the means which God would use

70

to hasten the day when all his hopes would be fulfilled. And that glorious fruition which was still in prospect filled his heart with ardent desire.

The hint of tension in that phrase *if by any means* is the key to the words that follow: It is 'not that I have already obtained or am already made perfect: but I press on, if so be that I may apprehend that for which also I was apprehended by Christ Jesus' (3:12). Paul was an utter realist; that is why he caught up the thought from the last verse and made his own practical attitude so clear. The goal he had in view, the full and final perfection, would only be achieved at the resurrection. He had not reached that goal nor grasped that prize: not yet; but he knew that there are lesser goals of relative perfection to which he might attain long before that final event. Therefore he pressed on, like a man hot in pursuit, with his eyes on the goal marked out for him in God's mercy. The phrase *if so be* is like an echo of that other phrase *if by any means* and is meant to express his strong sense of purpose. His one thought was to press forward in the spirit of eager and earnest desire to grasp that for which he had been grasped by the hand of Christ Himself. His thoughts for a moment moved back from the spiritual pursuit in which he was engaged in order to recall what had happened in the encounter on the road to Damascus and what was God's purpose in it. The Greek text was terse and compressed, but his meaning was clear. It was as though he had been placed under arrest, *apprehended*, by the hand of God in order to snatch him from ruin; as a result, his whole life had been turned round and was bent to the pursuit of one supreme ideal. He strove to grasp, to make his own, to *apprehend*, the crown of God's purpose for him. What had happened to him only served to dig the spur of resolution into his soul so as to make him press forward.

There is a strong personal emphasis in the deliberate repetition of this idea: 'Brethren, I count not myself yet to have apprehended: but one thing I do, forgetting the things which are behind and stretching forward to the things which are before' (3:13). The word *brethren* stands first as an appeal and to awaken interest. He was deeply moved as he spoke; what he said was clipped and abrupt. This was his own self-estimate, and it left no room for complacency. The verb was left without an object; this must be supplied from the context. He did not count himself to have grasped all that God had in store; *not yet*. He was nevertheless a man who lived for a single purpose: *but one thing I do*. Those five monosyllabic Anglo-Saxon words muster only fourteen letters in order to convey intense emotional feeling; but the Greek text requires only two words of four letters in all. *One thing* possessed his heart, dominated his mind, and ruled his life. That *one thing* was not defined; its meaning only becomes clear as the text unfolds. His words hurried on with almost insensible rapidity to take up a fresh and favourite metaphor. He was like an athlete who had to run the race God had marked out for him; and as he ran, he had to bear in mind the rules which were imperative for all earnest competitors. The first was to forget *the things which are behind*. He could not afford to look back over his shoulder; he could not live as it were in the past. So one experience after another was allowed to fall behind; he knew that it was what lay on ahead that would really matter. Therefore he stretched towards *the things which are before*. Straining every nerve and muscle, with his head thrown forward and his eyes on the goal, he ran as one whose whole being was at full stretch for God.

Those words cleared the ground and made room for the climax: 'I press on toward the goal unto the prize of the high calling of God in Christ Jesus' (3:14). The same Greek verb was used no less than three times in the course of this chapter, though more than one English word was used in the translation. It first occurs in Paul's striking account of his early career: 'As touching zeal, *persecuting* the church' (3:6). It was similarly employed in his address before Herod Agrippa: 'Being exceedingly mad against them, *I persecuted* them even unto foreign cities' (Acts 26:11). Then it occurs in his statement about pursuit of God's purpose: '*I press on, follow after* (A.V.), if so be that I may apprehend' (3:12). It is employed once more in this famous declaration: '*I press on* toward the goal' (3:14). It was a

word-picture borrowed from the hunt or from a foot-race, and
it was often coupled with that other word *apprehend*. They were
linked in the sense of to pursue and overtake or to chase and
capture.[1] So the tremendous fanatic zeal that once drove him
on in fierce persecution had now become harnessed to a nobler
purpose and he pressed toward the mark as one who was not to
be turned aside. He ran like Asahel in pursuit of Abner: he
was 'as light of foot as a wild roe', and turned neither to the
right hand nor to the left (2 Sam. 2:18). Or he ran like
Ahimaaz when he outran Cushi: he ran alone, and he brought
good tidings (2 Sam. 18:26). Paul had often referred to the
Greek games, and he likened himself to an athlete whose one
thought was to break the tape, and cross the line, and grasp
the prize. What did he mean by the prize of God's high calling?
What was the wreath, the victor's garland, which he had in
view? He did not say; but it must have been the surpassing
excellence of Christ Himself (cf. 3:8).

These words seem to form a natural conclusion to the
glorious rhetoric of his soaring aspiration, but he was still not
quite ready to give up the subject: 'Let us therefore, as many
as be perfect, be thus minded: and if in anything ye are
otherwise minded, even this shall God reveal unto you: only,
whereunto we have already attained, by that same rule let us
walk' (3:15-16). Paul wanted to identify himself with his
readers and to evoke in them the same lofty spiritual desires.
He sent their minds back to the word *perfect*, using it in the
sense of 'a maturity which ever seeks a fuller maturity' (cf.
3:12); it was relative perfection in the present circumstances of
life, not the absolute perfection which still belongs to the
future.[2] So let those who in this sense were perfect *be thus
minded*; let them share his resolve not to look back, but to press
on towards the goal. And if any were *otherwise minded*, he dared
to think that God would show them where they were at fault.
He would hardly have made mention of this had it not been for
the threat to corporate unity of which he was aware; it was in

[1] Ralph P. Martin, *ibid.* p. 152.
[2] Ralph P. Martin, *ibid.* p. 155.

fact a salutary but very gentle caution not to allow any selfish conceit to impede their pursuit of the prize of God's high calling. Then he nudged them with a final word of loving encouragement to go on as they had begun. The word *attained* is not the same as the word he had used before, and it implies the thought that it was not without difficulty that they had reached as far as was the case. Only therefore let them go on as far as their present insight allowed; only let them step out in faith by the same rule. By this gentle descent from the heights of splendid vision, Paul had reached this practical conclusion: those who walk in the light they have received may trust God to cause yet more light to shine on the path of inner understanding.

Paul had thus set out the qualities which are requisite for all who run that race with their eye on the goal; they are in fact implicit in the metaphor which he had used with such effect. It is hard to read this passage and to bear in mind the fact that the man who wrote it was climbing up in years, wearing on in life, in a prison cell and in chains. It reads like the language of a young man, standing on the threshold of life, ardent, eager and enthusiastic. But the fire that had been kindled on the road to Damascus continued to burn with as bright a flame as ever. He had been warned that bonds and trials would be his lot, but he was undeterred: 'None of these things move me, neither count I my life dear unto myself, so that I might finish my course with joy' (Acts 20:24 A.V.). Did he do it? The answer is supplied in the course of the last Letter he lived to write: 'I have fought the good fight; I have finished the course; I have kept the faith: henceforth there is laid up for me the crown of righteousness which the Lord, the righteous judge, shall give to me at that day' (2 Tim. 4:7-8). That has always been a tremendous stimulus for those who now run as he ran; and their encouragement may be all the greater for those who are growing old or nearing the end. So Charles Simeon at the age of 68 wrote with unselfconscious simplicity in the same strain: 'I seem to be so near the goal that I cannot but run with all my might'.[3] So too Mrs Howard Taylor at the age of 75 caught up the same great theme: 'I press on', she wrote; 'the finish is the thing; so many fail at the end'.[4] 'Therefore let us also, seeing we are compassed about with so great a cloud of witnesses, . . . run with patience the race that is set before us, looking unto Jesus . . . who for the joy that was set before Him, endured the cross, despising the shame, and hath sat down at the right hand of the throne of God'. (Heb. 12:1-2).

[3] William Carus: *Memoirs of The Life of The Rev. Charles Simeon*, 1847, p. 620.
[4] Joy Guinness: *Mrs Howard Taylor, Her Web of Time* p. 332.

Chapter Thirteen

Weakness All Mine, And Strength All Thine.

'I can do all things in him that strengtheneth me'
PHILIPPIANS 4:13.

THIS SHORT Letter moves to a close in terms of warm personal gratitude, though it begins at a distance from the object which was in mind. No church had done so much on Paul's behalf as the congregation at Philippi; they had sent more than once to help supply his needs during his initial visit to Thessalonica. Their love had been kindled afresh when they received the news of his imprisonment and they had sent Epaphroditus to seek him out with substantial proof of their loving concern. This was something which would touch all his own rich and generous sympathies and he wanted them to know what it meant to him: 'I rejoice in the Lord greatly, that now at length ye have revived your thought for me; wherein ye did indeed take thought, but ye lacked opportunity' (4:10). Paul was far more accustomed to give than to receive; it was a new thing to find that he was cast in the role of a recipient. He knew how his converts at Philippi had been forced to endure both poverty and privation; he had only felt able to accept their gifts because of the depth of their love. But it embarrassed him to receive these things at their expense, and he was more embarrassed when it came to voicing his thanks. He would have them know that he could have been content with or without such aid; it might enhance his joy, but that joy would not have vanished had he remained in more straitened circumstances: 'for I have learned, in whatsoever state I am, therein to be content' (4:11).

He knew 'in everything and in all things' how to be filled and how to be hungry, how to abound and how to be in want (4:12). His joy did not consist in gifts from friends or in material comforts at all; the secret lay elsewhere: 'I can do all things in him that strengtheneth me' (4:13).

These ten words in English, all monosyllabic but one, translate six words in Greek and are so well known that we may hardly welcome the thought of change. But they are a refreshing paraphrase rather than a literal translation, and a stricter reading will be found to hold an even richer content: 'I have strength for all things in union with Him who always makes me able'. This will enlarge the whole idea behind his words and will remove any thought of mere self-sufficiency. He had found a secret that would make him equal to all demands, whether that meant things he had to do or things he had to suffer. It is always much more easy to serve than to suffer, but his life was crowded with both. It is not too much to say that in all Christian history, no one has been called to do or to bear so much for Christ's sake as was he. There was enterprise, excitement, adventure; there was loneliness, privation, suffering: but he had learned to take all these things in his stride when they came in the will of God. He could attempt all things in the course of duty and service; he could endure all things in the path of hardship and ordeal. This is illustrated in the circumstances in which he was writing at that very moment, for he was an imperial prisoner, with chains on his wrists, hand-cuffed to a Roman soldier. No one can tell what a trial such imprisonment must have been for a man like Paul; but his spirit was free and his very bonds had fallen out for the furtherance of the Gospel. While that soldier was on duty, he was just as much a captive as Paul, and one by one every member of the praetorian guard had come to hear him speak of the Lord Jesus. There were saints in Caesar's household as a result of his faithful testimony, for he was strong for all things through One who never ceased to make him able (cf. 1:12-13).

This text held the secret that made Cromwell the chief captain and first ruler in the England of his own times. Thomas

Carlyle says that it was probably during 1623 that his conversion took place. The times were dark both at home and abroad; England stood in dire need of a good and brave man. All men saw the need; no one saw the man. But that man in God's good purpose would prove to be Cromwell and that began to make itself clear in 1643 when he formed the Ironsides. 'I had rather have a plain russet-coated captain', he wrote, 'that knows what he fights for and loves what he knows, than that which you call a Gentleman, and is nothing else.'[1] His first major battle was at Marston Moor in July 1644 and he won a decisive victory. But there was loss as well, and after the battle, he wrote to his brother-in-law, Colonel Valentine Walton: 'Sir, God hath taken away your eldest son by a cannon-shot . . . you know my own trials this way'. Walton knew that Cromwell had lost his own eldest son when not quite eighteen years old in May 1639 and that his second son had been killed in action not long before Marston Moor. That brief allusion to his bereavements paved the way for words of comfort to his brother-in-law in the loss of his son: 'He was a gallant young man, exceedingly gracious. God give you His comfort . . . You may do all things by the strength of Christ. Seek that, and you shall easily bear your trial'.[2] When in 1653 Cromwell became Lord Protector of England, a king in all but name, this text was still his strength: for the very word *king* comes from an old Saxon word which denotes *the man who can*. 'My burden is not ordinary,' he told his sister, 'nor are my weaknesses a few to go through therewith; but I have hope in a better strength'.[3] That text had come to his rescue like an army to the relief of a beleagured garrison, for he was strong to do all and dare all in the strength of that Other who stood by his side.

The first part of this verse was the simple declaration that Paul was strong for all things; the next clause set out the secret of that amazing confidence. It is significant that the name of Christ is not found in the Greek text, but there is not the least

[1] Thomas Carlyle, *ibid*. Letter XVI Vol. I. p. 147.
[2] *Ibid*. Letter XXI Vol. I pp. 166–167.
[3] *Ibid*. Appendix No. 23, Vol. V. p. 213.

shadow of doubt as to whom the words apply: 'I have strength for all things in union with Him who always makes me able'. Paul did not brace himself with some kind of Stoic resolution in order to contend with difficulty or adversity; he did not try to draw upon hidden reserves in the depths of his own spirit. He knew how his own strength was prone to turn into weakness in the midst of trial and ordeal; he was in fact deeply aware of the need and weakness in which he stood when he was left to stand alone. But he had an unshaken confidence in the God whose he was and whom he served, and he was sure that His grace was more than a match for all demands. Neither his own weakness nor the strength of adversity really mattered if the power of Christ were to rest on him, for he had found that in virtue of his union with Christ he drew on a boundless store of strength and sufficiency. This is also illustrated in the circumstances in which he was writing at that very moment, for his trial was moving to a climax and he was on the eve of a verdict. The long suspense was now almost over, though the issue still hung in the balance. He summed up the alternatives in order to assess his own feelings. He might be acquitted: his chains would be struck off and he would go out free. He might be condemned: he would hear the sentence of death and be led out to die at the point of a soldier's sword. How did he feel in the face of uncertainty? Was he anxious, or nervous, or apprehensive? No, not at all; for he was strong for all things through One who never ceased to make him able (cf. 1:19-24).

The text that armed Paul with strength was to arm Cromwell likewise in the gravest crises of life and death. When his eldest son died at school in May 1639, he was sorrow-stricken in a more than ordinary degree. We do not know the story; he was too grieved to tell the tale. There is only the one transient reference to it in his letter to his brother-in-law, Colonel Walton. Cromwell loved his sons and daughters very dearly; he was described by a friend as looking 'sad and wearied' on the eve of Marston Moor, having heard of the death of his second son in battle not long before.[4] Those sorrows lay buried too

[4] Thomas Carlyle, *ibid*. Vol. II p. 265.

deep for words almost to the end of his life. Then came July 1658 when his favourite daughter, Elizabeth Claypole, was desperately ill at Hampton Court. She was in fact dying from a painful form of cancer as July passed into August; there was nothing he could do to save her. Andrew Marvell left a vivid picture of the dying girl as she tried to hide her pain so as not to alarm her father, while Cromwell tried to hide his anguish lest he should add to her distress: but they knew each other too well, and the effort only left them drained and weary.[5] She died on August 6th, and he never recovered. The old sorrow seems to have been freshened by her terrible suffering; it was to surge into his mind in his final illness as that month ran its course. He called for his Bible and asked someone to read this text once more. 'This Scripture', he said, 'did once save my life, when my eldest son died; which went as a dagger to my heart, indeed it did'. He mused on Paul's words and said the verse to himself. Then faith began to work, and his heart to find comfort and support, and he said thus to himself, 'He that was Paul's Christ is my Christ too'. and so drew waters out of the well of salvation.[6] The words which had brought him courage in youth and comfort in sorrow held to the end, and he was strong to brave all and bear all in the strength of that Other who stood by his side.

This verse should arm our souls with strength as it armed both Paul and Cromwell: 'I can do all things in him that strengtheneth me'. Paul knew what it was to endure a thorn in the flesh: this must have been something painful, something chronic, and something which in his eyes was a serious handicap to his personal ministry. It was almost more than he could bear and he besought the Lord, not once, nor twice, but three times to take it away. That did not happen, but he heard the voice of Jesus say: 'My grace! My grace is sufficient; My grace is sufficient for thee' (2 Cor. 12:9). What did infirmity, or insult, or hardship, or persecution matter if the power of Christ were to rest on him? 'For when I am weak, then I am strong' (2 Cor.

[5] Antonia Fraser: Cromwell Our Chief of Men p. 666.
[6] Thomas Carlyle, ibid. Vol. V pp. 148–149.

12:10). And what he had found in his own experience he longed to share with his converts: 'For this cause', he wrote, 'I bow my knees unto the Father . . . that He would grant you . . . that ye may be *strengthened with power* through His Spirit in the inward man' (Eph. 3:14-16). So he exhorted Timothy: 'Thou therefore, my child, be strengthened (*strengthen thyself*) in the grace that is in Christ Jesus' (2 Tim. 2:1). What of ourselves today? We may have duty, or hardship, or difficulty to face; we may have trouble, or sorrow, or disappointment to bear. There may be times when we feel so weak in ourselves that we hardly know how to see things through. And yet, if we only grasp the truth of this text by faith, we shall learn how to bear that trial: He will grant us to be strengthened with grace by means of His Spirit in the inmost region of our being. For why should not Paul's Christ be our Christ too? And why should not the grace that was sufficient for him be equal to all our need?

Chapter Fourteen

Our Redemption

'In whom we have our redemption through his blood,
the forgiveness of our trespasses, according to the riches
of his grace'.

ＥＰＨＥＳＩＡＮＳ 1:7

THIS LETTER was almost certainly intended as a general
circular for the churches in the Roman Province of Asia.
Ephesus was the capital of the Province and lent its name to
the copy preserved in the Canon. This explains the special
form of address in the salutation and the absence of all personal
reference in the contents of the Letter. He wrote to *the saints* in
each church whose name was filled in where the word *Ephesus*
stands, and to all *the faithful* in the other churches of the
Province: 'Paul, an apostle of Christ Jesus through the will of
God, to the saints which are at Ephesus, and the faithful in
Christ Jesus: grace to you and peace from God our Father and
the Lord Jesus Christ' (1:1-2). Then he launched out in a
passage that would lift their eyes to the most lofty plateau of
divine purpose and blessing; God has blessed us with all
spiritual blessings in heavenly places in Christ (1:3). Would
his readers pause when they heard those words? Would they
wonder how all this could have come to be? God had chosen
them 'before the foundation of the world'; He had foreordained
them to become as sons in His household (1:4-5). So Paul
declared; and yet what were they that, 'in an eternity above all
time', they should have been so richly favoured?[1] The grace of
God was the unique secret that lay at the heart of this claim.
It was 'to the praise of the glory of his grace' (1:6); it was

[1] H. C. G. Moule: *Ephesian Studies* p. 30.

'according to the riches of his grace' (1:8). The old English
Version declares that it was grace 'wherein he hath made us
accepted in the beloved' (1:6 A.V.). But the Revised Version
more correctly translates it as 'which he freely bestowed on us
in the beloved'. This means that God has been gracious towards
us in virtue of our union with the Son of His love. The whole
context suggests that this is the grace that makes us welcome
in God's presence; God treats us with His rich unmerited
favour because we are *in the beloved*.

The long soaring sentence descends at last from the eternal
covenant to the historic transaction: 'In whom we have our
redemption through his blood, the forgiveness of our trespasses,
according to the riches of his grace' (1:7). *Redemption* was a
term which owed its origin to the market place where slaves or
captives of war could be redeemed, set free, by the payment of
a ransom. This meant something more than the bare fact of
ransom or of release: it meant release which had been brought
about as a direct result of the payment of a ransom. A synonym
for *redemption* was coined by H. C. G. Moule in the term
ransom-rescue; and that hyphenated term combines the ideas of
ransom and release.[2] Those only are redeemed who have first
been ransomed, and then as a result have been released. That
deliverance from bondage and restoration to freedom is all
implicit in *our redemption*. Paul took the term which had been
in use for ages, and then applied its full spiritual significance
to these Gentile converts. They knew as well as he did that all
men are by nature slaves or captives of sin: they may long for
freedom, but there is no way in which they can free themselves.
They can not buy their own release; nothing they do can earn
the right to shake off their chains and to go out free. Logic and
law compel us to see that no one is self-redeemed; we can never
secure our own deliverance. But what men can not do through
their own self-effort, the Son of God has done on their behalf.
He was made our wisdom both for righteousness and for
holiness, and all that is summed up in the word *redemption* (cf.
1 Cor. 1:30). He is the One *in whom* we have all that

[2] H. C. G. Moule: The *Epistle to The Romans* (*The Expositor's Bible*) p. 92.

redemption represents, and all this is an act of grace on God's part for Christ's sake alone.

The argument is different, but the same thought occurs elsewhere: we are 'justified freely by his grace through the redemption that is in Christ Jesus' (Rom 3:24). The full context in each case makes it clear that there was a ransom. It was paid 'through his blood' (Eph. 1:7 cf. Rom. 3:25); that is, on the ground of His death. The most striking element in the redemption of Israel from Egypt was blood, shed and sprinkled. That blood was the symbol of death; it meant that life had been poured out. Israel had become a redeemed people because they were under that blood. This was applied in a still more impressive ritual to the deliverance of those who were guilty under the law. The whole system of man's approach to God, whether in tabernacle or temple, was based on the demand for sacrifice and atonement. The law was quite explicit in its requirements; it is summed up in one famous saying: 'All things are cleansed with blood, and apart from shedding of blood there is no remission' (Heb. 9:22 R.V.). Death had to be endured, or there could be no peace with God; and the sign of that death was the shedding of blood. Therefore in the fulness of time, God sent His Son in the likeness of men, and that ransom was paid once and for all when His blood was shed on the cross. He 'made peace', so Paul wrote, 'through the blood of his cross' (Col. 1:20). That was the price which He paid down for our deliverance from the guilt and bondage of sin, and the double idea of ransom and rescue tells what it means to be redeemed. So Peter wrote: 'Ye were redeemed, not with corruptible things, with silver or gold, . . . but with precious blood, as of a lamb without blemish and without spot, even the blood of Christ' (1 Pet. 1:18-19).

The rest of Paul's sentence in this great verse is in apposition with and explanation of the first half: 'the forgiveness of our trespasses, according to the riches of his grace' (1:7). *Forgiveness* is seen as one of the primary benefits of our redemption, though it does not exhaust all that it means to be redeemed. It is a term which owed its origin to the arrangements for a year of

Jubilee; that is, a year of release from the cumulative debts of half a century (cf. Lev. 25:31 LXX). So God forgives in order to release men from the debt they owe to Him, and the cause of that debt is the endless series of sins by which they have fallen short of His just demands. The word *trespass* points to any deviation from the straight line drawn by the will of God; to turn to the right or the left even for a moment is to leave the highway God has marked out for us. Such a deviation may take place in the mind even when there is no act of trespass in conduct or practice. There is no man who can plead that he is not guilty to the charge that he has erred times without number. 'All we like sheep have gone astray; we have turned every one to his own way' (Isa. 53:6). *Our trespasses* must stand condemned for what they are; they are sins, and each sin adds to that vast burden of debt under which we labour. It is only God who can cancel the debt and forgive the sin, and nothing can exaggerate our need in each respect. The two ideas of *debts* and *sins* are made clear in the two versions of the Lord's Prayer: 'Forgive us our debts' (Matt. 6:12); 'forgive us our sins' (Luke 11:4). That *forgiveness* was one supreme object in view when the Son of Man went up to die in Jerusalem. 'This is my blood', He said, '. . . which is shed for many unto *remission* (forgiveness) of sins'. (Matt. 26:28).

The whole verse is almost identical with a sentence in the Epistle to the Colossians: 'In whom we have our redemption, the forgiveness of our sins' (Col. 1:14). This verse omits the phrase 'through his blood'; it employs the word *sins* instead of *trespasses*; and it leaves out the final reference to 'the riches of his grace'. But it speaks of redemption and of forgiveness in the same terms and in the same relationship. The Old Testament refers to the forgiving love of God in a great variety of metaphors. 'The Lord is slow to anger and plenteous in mercy, forgiving iniquity and transgression' (Num. 14:18; cf. Exod. 34:6-7). He will put our sins from us as far as the east is from the west (Ps. 103:12). He casts them all behind His back (Isa. 38:17); He blots them out as with a cloud (Isa. 44:22). They are thrust out of mind and memory (Jer. 31:34); they are buried in the depths of the sea (Mic. 7:19). And what God has buried at the bottom of the sea will never be washed up on the shore. It may seem all the more strange that Paul so seldom spoke of forgiveness. He used the noun itself in only two other contexts: each was in the course of a speech. In the synagogue of Antioch of Pisidia, he said: 'Be it known unto you therefore, brethren, that through this man is proclaimed unto you remission (forgiveness) of sins' (Acts 13:38). And he told Herod Agrippa that part of his commission to the Gentiles was 'to open their eyes . . . that they may receive remission (forgiveness) of sins' (Acts 26:18). But the meaning of that word was absorbed in the larger ideas of justification and reconciliation, and they teach us to say with David: 'There is forgiveness with thee, that thou mayest be feared' (Ps. 130:4). This is what H. C. G. Moule has described as God's 'wonderful amnesty' for the sinner:[3] He cancels our debt, forgives our sin, and redeems our soul from death.

The text concludes with a comment on the ultimate origin of this mercy: it was 'according to', on the immense scale of, 'the riches of his grace'. The word *riches* was one of Paul's favourite expressions in his untiring endeavour to show the reach of God's love and goodness. He is rich in mercy (2:4), rich in grace (2:7), rich in glory (3:16), rich in Christ (3:8); we can never come to the end of the riches which are stored up in God's loving purpose for all who share in His sovereign redemption. Here the particular application of this word is to the boundless wealth of God's grace. The word *grace* means loving kindness; it will always speak of God's most gracious favour. Therefore when God forgives the debt we owe, it is an act of grace. Nothing that we can do is good enough to earn God's love for us; we can never lay claim to it as though it were something we have deserved. It is beyond the reach of all human effort, because all our obedience bears the mark of imperfection. Grace has nothing in common with ideas of merit and reward; it is God's free gift for those who are in themselves totally undeserving. There is no cause for it in us

[3] H. C. G. Moule: *Ephesian Studies* p. 32.

apart from our own desperate need; there is no cause for it in
God apart from His own generous love. This great doctrine of
grace lies at the heart of all Pauline theology; nothing separated
him so sharply from the Jews of that age. But *the riches of His
grace* were equally relevant to the Gentiles; there was no ground
apart from this on which they could hope to be made welcome
in the presence of God. It is in Christ alone that God provides
for redemption and forgiveness; this is the same for the Gentile
as for the Jew. It is an act of grace, and that grace is always
available in God, always accessible in Christ.

Chapter Fifteen

The Grace and Gift of God

'For by grace have ye been saved through faith; and that
not of yourselves: it is the gift of God: not of works, that
no man should glory'.

EPHESIANS 2:8-9

PAUL HAD begun to set out God's magnificent design for His
redeemed people in words that lift our eyes beyond time to
eternity: 'that in the ages to come he might shew the exceeding
riches of his grace in kindness toward us in Christ Jesus' (2:7).
God's plan reaches beyond the great events of the resurrection
and the exaltation of Christ; beyond the fact of our spiritual
union with Him in this mighty experience; beyond 'this world'
to 'that which is to come' (cf. 1:21). This is partly explained
by his later declaration that God had done all things 'to the
intent that now unto the principalities and the powers in the
heavenly places might be made known through the church the
manifold wisdom of God' (3:10). This would be the crowning
display of His grace in all its *exceeding riches*. He was more than
ready to strain all the powers of human language in order to
convey a just sense of the truth, and he alone among New
Testament writers made use of this superlative term *exceeding*.
He used it twice in his Second Letter to the Church at Corinth
(2 Cor. 3:10; 9:14), and no less than three times in this Letter
(1:19; 2:7; 3:19). That grace had been expressed in His *kindness
toward us in Christ Jesus*. The same idea occurs in a phrase which
makes it clear that *kindness* denotes love in action: 'When the
kindness of God our Saviour, and his love toward man,
appeared' (Titus 3:4). The full impact of the whole verse is felt
at once by a contrast with the tenor of the first part of this

passage. The resurrection and exaltation of Christ were the supreme demonstration of 'the exceeding greatness of his power' (1:19); and the union of His people with Him in this mighty experience is the supreme demonstration of 'the exceeding riches of his grace' (2:7).

Paul went on to take up the word *grace* which he had just used and in addition to repeat a phrase which had slipped in as a parenthesis as his argument unfolded: 'For by grace have ye been saved through faith' (2:8; cf. 2:5). The word *for* makes it clear that this verse is firmly linked with all that had gone before, and the definite article in Greek before the word *grace* helps to show that it refers to that grace which he had already foreshadowed (cf. 2:5, 7). The God who is 'rich in mercy' (2:4) is no less rich in grace (2:7); and grace is the free and boundless favour of God. Such grace is the ground of all God's action 'for us men and for our salvation':[1] it flows from the mercy of God, and not from our human merit. Grace is a king's largesse for the needy; it is a royal reprieve for the guilty. Grace came where sin had come and reached out its hand to man where he had fallen so that he might be *saved*. Salvation is a word which implies the dual thought of danger and of rescue. Israel was saved from the might of Pharaoh when the gravest danger threatened and when they were rescued by the arm of God's strength. Men are in danger of death and hell; they need the rescue of grace and God. No doubt in the context of this passage the word was used with the widest meaning: it was meant to cover the whole process of man's rescue from the consequences of sin in all forms and aspects. The verb in its perfect tense was meant to express something which was present but which had come about as the result of past action; something which was both an accomplished reality and a continuing process. It is by grace that men have been and are being saved; and the means by which this rescue takes place is *faith*.

The next words are meant to define, with a decisive clarity, what is unique in this experience: 'And that, not of yourselves:

[1] The Nicene Creed.

it is the gift of God'. There can be no doubt as to the primary emphasis of this statement, but a minor problem is posed by one detail. The key word *that* is a demonstrative pronoun in the neuter gender: to what does it refer? It may refer to the whole idea of a free salvation as the basic theme in this verse, and this could be expressed in an amplified paraphrase: 'you have been saved as an act of grace and by means of faith: and that tremendous salvation did not spring from yourselves; it is the gift of God'. This view derives support from the fact that the phrase *not of yourselves* is a parallel utterance with the phrase *not of works* in the next verse; and that verse must be read as an ultimate reference to the whole concept of a free salvation. But the alternative to this is that the real antecedent of that demonstrative pronoun is the word *faith* and that the clause as a whole is a fresh parenthesis (cf. 2:5). This is perhaps best set out by means of another paraphrase: 'You have been saved by grace alone, in Christ alone, through faith alone: and that very faith is not of yourselves; it is the gift of God'. The word *faith* is feminine in contrast with the neuter gender of the pronoun; but Paul had used the phrase *and that*, in the neuter gender, elsewhere to bring in a new thought which would heighten all that had gone before (cf. 1 Cor. 6:6, 8; Phil. 1:28). If the pronoun refers only to the basic concept of a free salvation, it adds no fresh significance to the original statement that it was all an act of grace. But if it is meant to take up the phrase *through faith*, it is seen to mark a distinct advance with its declaration that faith itself must be given of God. Salvation as a whole is an act of grace, and the very faith that makes it ours is *the gift of God*.

This view allows us to read the verse as a whole with a richer insight into God's great purpose for man in Christ: 'For by grace have ye been saved through faith: and that [faith is] not of yourselves; it is the gift of God'. *Faith* is the one link in this chain which men might have thought they could forge for themselves, but these words show that men can do nothing at all to win salvation as a recompense for virtue or merit. We may trace back the work of God in our lives as far as we can go in conscious recollection; we may suppose that it began with a crisis moment of faith, or trust, or personal surrender, or decisive commitment. But we need to inquire as to what lay behind that first conscious response. Faith can not be generated by an act of self-volition; it is impossible for a man to create true faith at will. Such faith does not depend on human understanding and can not be derived from mental effort. We can not make ourselves have faith in God; we are as much in need in this respect as in all else. Faith can only originate in man's heart as the gift of God. Paul had stated this in terms of singular interest in a practical connection: 'Unto you *it is given* in the behalf of Christ . . . *to believe* on Him' (Phil. 1:29 A.V.). That phrase is, if anything, emphasised in the Revised Version: 'To you it hath been granted . . . to believe on Him'. This does not mean that God engenders some new faculty in us that was not there before: it means that grace prevails in our inmost spirit so that we put our trust in Him as we did not before. Faith is therefore as much the gift of God to His people as 'repentance . . . and remission of sins' (Acts 5:31): God so opens the eyes of the mind that we can do no other than trust in Him.

The last phrase caught up the main theme in a final emphatic utterance to show that it is by grace and through faith alone that men are saved: 'not of works, that no man should glory' (2:9). The term *works* is like an echo of the language in Romans and Galatians where the works of the law were the vital issue in the eyes of the Jew. Sometimes *works* were spoken of in contrast with grace (cf. Rom. 11:16); and sometimes in contrast with faith (cf. Rom. 4:5). If such works could accrue merit in God's sight and in God's judgment, then men would not be saved by grace alone, through faith alone. People in all ages like to think that there is something which they can do, or some contribution which they should make, so that they can be saved. The last stronghold they are willing to let go is the proud independence which leads them to suppose that they can make themselves worthy. If this were true, even in the smallest degree, they would have grounds for self-glory and

would be free to boast (cf. Rom. 4:2). But that is not the case;
Paul knew better; his own experience taught him that to boast
is worthless. The voice of the veteran Puritan, Stephen
Charnock, may well be heard on this matter. 'What are a few
tears but a drop to our sea of guilt?' he wrote; 'what are our
petitions but as the breath of a child to the storms of our
provocations? our righteousness but as a mite to the many
talents of our unrighteousness? Sinful duties can not make an
infinite and holy satisfaction'.[2] Augustus Montague Toplady
proclaimed the same truth in words which are now part of our
rich Christian heritage:

> Not the labours of my hands
>   Can fulfil Thy law's demands;
> Could my zeal no respite know,
>   Could my tears for ever flow,
> All for sin could not atone;
>   Thou must save, and Thou alone.[3]

Paul could write in those terms from the heart with calm
and sober reality; he could tell his readers that by the grace of
God and through the gift of faith, they had been saved indeed.
This has been no less true for men in all ages once they have
seen that the vast gulf between God and man can be bridged
by God alone. Such a discovery was made by John Charles Ryle
when he sauntered into church one Sunday morning while the
Service was in progress. He felt depressed with the approach of
his final exams for an honours degree, and was so far oblivious
of the world at large that he could never recall just which
church in Oxford it was. The prayers were read by a stranger,
and he forgot the text of the sermon; but he had come in and
taken his seat just in time to hear the second lesson. This came
from the second chapter in the Epistle to The Ephesians. It was
read with uncommon earnestness; two verses in particular were
read with an impressive emphasis which he could not ignore.
There was a pause between each phrase as though to let each

---

[2] Stephen Charnock: *Complete Works* (Edited by James M'Cosh) Vol. III p. 303.
[3] A. M. Toplady: Hymn 579 in *The Book of Common Praise*.

new concept sink down into the minds of the hearers: 'For by grace . . . are ye saved . . . through faith; . . . and that, not of yourselves: . . . it is the gift of God: . . . not of works . . . lest any man should boast' (A.V.). Ryle must have heard those words often enough before, but their point had been dulled by the confused murmur of the world all around. But that morning, in the silence of each fresh pause, the still small voice of God spoke to his heart. He heard that voice in a way that awoke the power of faith with an immediate response to the grace and mercy of God. Faith is like the hand of a beggar, empty, open, and outstretched to receive; and it was the simple hearing of those words of Scripture that led him to stretch out his hand and grasp the gift of salvation.[4]

[4] M. L. Loane: *Makers of Our Heritage* p. 24; cf. J. S. Reynolds: *Canon Christopher of St Aldate's Oxford* p. 144.

Chapter Sixteen

To the Gentiles

'Unto me, who am less than the least of all saints, was this grace given, to preach unto the Gentiles the unsearchable riches of Christ'.

EPHESIANS 3:8

THIS CHAPTER had begun with words which were meant to form a preface for the heartfelt supplication of a man on his knees at prayer: 'For this cause, I Paul, the prisoner of Christ Jesus in behalf of you Gentiles' (3:1). The *cause* he had in mind was the sovereign indwelling of God in His people (cf. 2:22); and that habitation of God by means of His Spirit in the church at large was equivalent to the habitation of Christ by the same means in their own hearts (cf. 3:17). Paul's plan was to apply this thought in a particular way to every Gentile convert and he began with a sensitive reference to the fact that he was now in prison on their behalf. But the very mention of *you Gentiles* broke up his train of thought. His mind raced off at a tangent in order to expand on God's purpose for the Gentiles, and he spoke at length of *the mystery of Christ*, God's great open secret, withheld from the knowledge of so many ages, but now revealed for all to know (cf. 3:4-5). This was nothing less than the fact that *the Gentiles* could now partake of 'the promise in Christ Jesus through the gospel', and he was a living agent of that message by the gift and the grace of God (cf. 3:6-7). This text lies at the heart of this long and typical digression: 'Unto me, who am less than the least of all saints, was this grace given, to preach unto the Gentiles the unsearchable riches of Christ' (3:8). But a question at once occurs: on which clause of this verse was the primary emphasis meant to fall? Was it his self-designation as one who was *less than the least*?

94

Or was it his declaration on *the unsearchable riches of Christ*? It was neither; it was the fact that such a man as he had been chosen to preach these things to *the Gentiles*.

It will be best to treat each clause in the order in which it comes: 'Unto me, who am less than the least of all saints'. Paul was so deeply moved that he described himself by a double diminutive; he had to coin a word for the purpose. He chose a word in the superlative degree and then raised it to a further comparative. He did not feel content to speak of himself as *the least*; he was even *less than the least*. This was a breach of the rules of grammar, but what did that matter when he had to express such intensity of feeling? This line of thought may be compared with his statement in a different connection: 'I am *the least* of the apostles, that am not meet to be called an apostle, because I persecuted the church of God' (1 Cor. 15:9). He could never thank 'Christ Jesus our Lord' enough in view of the fact that he had been called as one of His servants (1 Tim. 1:12). And why? Because he could never forget what he had been before: 'a blasphemer, and a persecutor, and injurious' (1 Tim. 1:13). But he had found mercy, and he summed it all up in a faithful saying that was worthy of all acceptation: 'Christ Jesus came into the world to save sinners' of whom he was the chief (1 Tim. 1:15). There was no mock self-abasement in that saying; it was the voice of the deepest humility. He could only think of himself as the worst of sinners, the one who was foremost of all in guilt. But he was not consciously comparing himself in this verse with others, either with fellow servants or fellow sinners; he was simply speaking as one who felt overwhelmed by the majesty of grace which had placed him among *all saints*. He had been the *chief* of sinners; how could he be other than the *least* of all saints? But that did not go far enough. Think of *the least*; he was even *less than* the least.

Paul moved swiftly forward to the main thrust of his declaration: 'Unto me . . . was this grace given'. He was overwhelmed by the magnitude of the mercy God had bestowed on him. It drove him to his knees, with his hand on his mouth and his mouth in the dust. He knew that he had no standing, no merit, no talent, that could make him worthy of the least of all God's mercies; but *grace* had been *given* to him. Grace would not have been grace if it had not been free; he could not have received it at all if it were not as a gift. There is similar emphasis in his crucial statement on the subject of man's acceptance with God: we are 'justified *freely*, by his *grace*' (Rom. 3:24). It was as though he looked to the sinner and said: This is all free; it is a gift which has nothing to do with ideas of a just payment. And then he looked to the Saviour and said: This is by grace; it is a grant which has nothing to do with ideas of a just reward. Both ideas are present in this declaration. The grant he had received could only refer to something which from God's point of view was to be seen as grace-wise, and from man's point of view as gift-wise. Paul knew that in himself he had nothing, and was no one at all; and for others, he had nothing apart from what he had received. But grace, *this grace* which he had been given, was for the sake of others. This once bigoted Pharisee, fanatic, blasphemer; this man whose hands wore the stains of Stephen's blood had yet found mercy; it was given to him to stand as a living witness to grace. How could he be silent? It was the same with John Newton when he was urged to give up preaching on account of his age and infirmity. 'What?' he said. 'Shall the old African blasphemer stop while he can speak?'[1]

This grace had been given with one particular object in view: it was that he should 'preach unto the Gentiles'. It is impossible to over-estimate or over-emphasise the strength of his feeling on this subject. He had discovered on the road to Damascus that God's plan was that he should go to the Gentiles, 'to open their eyes that they may turn from darkness to light' (Acts 26:18). Such a plan would be as revolutionary in his eyes as in the eyes of any orthodox Pharisee, but he was to devote his life to the cause of missionary evangelism on their behalf. It was true that he could never really dislodge his own sense of surprise that the grace of God should reach out beyond Jewish circles to them also. He was far more conscious of the wonder of God's mercy towards them

---

[1] *An Authentic Narrative of the Life of John Newton*, written by himself; with a continuation by the Rev. Richard Cecil p. 147.

than they were themselves, and it always seemed to call for comment in ways that must have brought a smile to those who knew him well. But his dedication to the Gentiles was an endless source of trouble for him where the Jews were concerned. This was sharply illustrated in his speech from the steps of the Castle Antonia after he had been snatched from death by the band of Roman soldiers. The Jews who had almost lynched him listened in deep silence as he told his story. He held back nothing from them as he described the great encounter on the road to Damascus, and they heard it without interruption. But the climax came when he told them of the charge which God had laid on him: 'Depart, for I will send thee forth far hence unto the Gentiles' (Acts 22:21). *The Gentiles!* Pandemonium broke out at that word. They threw off their cloaks, flung dust in the air, and yelled for his death: 'Away with such a fellow from the earth; for it is not fit that he should live' (Acts 22:22). And all this arose from his call to preach to *the Gentiles*.

And what was he to preach to the Gentiles? Just what he would preach to the Jews, namely, 'the unsearchable riches of Christ'. Six times in this Letter he wrote of the *riches* that may be found in God, riches beyond all human telling, beyond all finite understanding. God is rich in mercy (2:4); rich in grace (1:7; 2:7); and rich in glory (1:18; 3:16); and it is all summed up in this phrase about 'the unsearchable riches of Christ'. He used another adjective which was calculated to stretch mind and imagination to the utmost limit: *unsearchable*, untrackable, something that can not be traced by human footprints. Job had voiced his thoughts long before, making use of the same term: 'As for me, I would seek unto God, and unto God would I commit my cause: which doeth great things and *unsearchable*; marvellous things without number' (Job 5:8-9). He could not let the thought vanish, but came back to it in a later account of God's greatness: He 'doeth great things *past finding out*; yea, marvellous things without number' (Job 9:10). It was like the Psalmist who stood as it were on the shore, looking out across the waters of a vast and immeasurable sea: 'Thy way was in the sea, and thy paths in the great waters, and thy footsteps were not known' (Ps. 77:19). But Paul applied that thought, not as Job did to the great things which God had done, nor as the Psalmist did to those footsteps which could not be traced in the great waters, but to all the riches of God which are summed up in Christ Himself. He had been put in trust with the Gospel; his call was to preach Christ to the Gentiles; all His unsearchable riches were now available for them on the same terms as for the Jews.

The word *unsearchable* suggests something that is as much beyond human comprehension as God's footprints in the great deep; it is used in this verse to hint at wealth beyond human understanding in the Person of Christ. During the last World War, a London jewel merchant found it hard to arrange for the sale of two twenty-five carat rubies which had come into his hands. But he had heard that the Nizam of Hyderabad was a man of vast wealth with a special flair for such gems, and he hoped to persuade him to buy them. A visit was arranged, and the merchant told his story. Then he took the rubies out of an inner pocket and placed them on the table. Nothing was said for a moment; their beauty and lustre spoke for themselves. But the Nizam saw them without surprise, and a servant was sent out to bring back a large steel trunk. This was unlocked in his presence; it was full of little leather bags, each with a ring round its neck. He picked up one, removed the ring, and poured out the contents. There were some two dozen rubies, far more lovely and more precious than the two gems which the merchant had brought. Then he opened another bag and poured out a handful of emeralds; then another which was full of pearls; and so on, until almost every kind of gem lay before his eyes. Nor was this all; when the Nizam spoke at last, it was to tell the merchant that there were still many more trunks in the palace strong-room; they were all filled with stones like these.[2] This would represent fabulous treasure in the eyes of that English merchant with his pair of rubies; yet what was all this in comparison with 'the unsearchable riches of Christ'? And those riches are for all men, Jew and Gentile, if they only believe.

[2] D. F. Karaka: *Fabulous Mogul* (Nizam VII of Hyderabad) pp. 61–63.

Chapter Seventeen

A Vocation to Holiness

'I therefore, the prisoner in the Lord, beseech you to
walk worthily of the calling wherewith ye were called'.
EPHESIANS 4:1-3

PAUL HAD addressed himself in the first half of this Letter to an
exposition of the doctrines of grace; in the latter half, the direction and emphasis of his thinking was on rules of conduct. It is
common to find in the structure of his Letters that he dealt with
matters of doctrine and conduct in that order, but no Letter is
more evenly divided for this purpose than the Epistle to The
Ephesians. Paul would never allow any separation of doctrine
from conduct; as a man thinks in his heart, so is he. Theology
must issue in practical holiness; conduct must be rooted and
grounded in doctrine. The great doxology at the end of the third
chapter must have been seen as a suitable conclusion for the first
half of this Letter, but the second section begins with a word
which marks the essential connection. *Therefore*, Paul wrote; what
I now have to say springs from all I have said. They had been
called to share God's great ransom-rescue as an act of His grace,
and they had been strengthened with might by means of His
Spirit so that Christ might dwell in their hearts by faith. *Therefore*
he would address this strong appeal to them as a personal
entreaty; he would have them listen to him as one who was now in
prison on their behalf. His doctrine and ethics were of one piece;
one had to lead to the other. He had taught them what to believe;
he would teach them how to behave. And the 'inter-texture'[1] of
the two halves reveals itself in the deliberate repetition of the
designation which he chose for himself: 'I Paul, the prisoner of

[1] H. C. G. Moule: *Ephesian Studies* p. 172.

Christ Jesus' (3:1); 'I therefore, the prisoner in the Lord' (4:1).
The effect is heightened in view of the fact that in the first case his
train of thought had been interrupted, and he resumed this form
of self-designation with a strong sense of continuity.

Paul launched this new appeal with a personal reference which
touched chords of simple pathos: 'I therefore, the prisoner in the
Lord, beseech you to walk worthily of the calling wherewith ye
were called' (4:1). He was in the prison quarters assigned to him,
handcuffed to a Roman soldier, never alone. There were chains
on his wrists; he was 'in bonds' (6:20 A.V.); he was denied all
privacy for communion in prayer. He bowed his knees in the
presence of his Father, but he had to kneel on the cold flag-stones
of his cell while the guard looked on, perhaps with cynical
unconcern, perhaps with wondering reverence. His trial had yet
to start; there was as yet neither condemnation, nor verdict, nor
sentence, and we can form little idea of what such an imprisonment must have cost him. But he did not refer to his circumstances in order to elicit sympathy; he had in fact foreseen that he
would be called to endure bonds and imprisonment, and he
would not allow such a prospect to make him flinch from the path
of duty; no, not for a single moment. He drew strength and
comfort from the knowledge that he was *in the Lord*; it was because
of this union with Christ that he had been called to suffer for
Him. This would colour his thinking and counsel to the close of
his life: 'All that would live godly in Christ Jesus shall suffer
persecution' (2 Tim. 3:12). But if we die with Him, then shall
we live with Him; if we endure, then shall we reign with Him. In
that, he could rejoice; he could glory in his chains more than a
king in his crown;[2] and that served to invest his words with the
authority of one whose life never seemed to vary in its steadfast
pursuit of God's great high calling.

But that self-reference was merged at once in his primary
objective: 'I therefore . . . beseech you to walk worthily of the
calling wherewith ye were called' (4:1). The word *walk* is used no
less than six times in the course of this Letter (2:2, 10; 4:1; 5:2,
8, 15), and in each case except the first it is applied with a positive

[2] Charles Hodge: *A Commentary on The Epistle to the Ephesians*, 1883, p. 140.

emphasis to a life of practical godliness. Its real origin as a metaphor goes back to the luminous description of the patriarch Enoch in the Book of Genesis: 'And Enoch walked with God: and he was not; for God took him' (Gen. 5:24). Later it was said of Noah: 'Noah was a righteous man, and perfect in his generations: Noah walked with God' (Gen. 6:9). Abram also heard the divine command: 'I am God Almighty; walk before me, and be thou perfect' (Gen. 17:1). The word may be employed in a spiritual sense to denote progress; a step-by-step advance towards the goal; but the aorist tense in this verse seems to indicate a new point of departure. It was as though Paul were to entreat his readers 'to set out on life's walk'[3] in a way that was in total contrast with their former manner of life when they had 'walked according to the course of this world' (2:2). He would have them commit themselves as though they were pilgrims to what would be a new journey, and they were to do this in a manner that was *worthy* of their calling in Christ. There was to be a true moral correspondence between their walk and its goal which he had spoken of as 'the hope of his calling' (1:18). This was comparable with an earlier entreaty: 'that ye should walk worthily of God, who calleth you into his own kingdom and glory' (1 Thess. 2:12). He had never lost sight of that need for moral integrity (cf. Phil. 1:27), nor of the goal towards which they should look with a steadfast intent (cf. Phil. 3:14).

This was a vocation to holiness; it would call for personal discipline: 'With all lowliness and meekness, with long-suffering, forbearing one another in love' (4:2). He had spoken of them as those who had been lifted from the depths of sin to the heights of glory (cf. 2:1-6), and their exaltation to the heavenlies made that call to holiness the more imperative. But how was such holiness to find expression in the terms of daily life and habit? Perhaps his answer would surprise those who only thought of a vague, scarcely defined ideal. It was a call for that kind of self-abasement which a vision of God's glory ought to inspire, and which would be founded on the conscious knowledge of the guilt and weakness that are ours by nature. The four virtues which he

[3] H. C. G. Moule, *ibid.* p. 173.

mentioned were arranged in congenial couplets: lowliness and
meekness; long-suffering and forbearance. Except for the substi-
tution of *humility* for *lowliness*, he linked the same virtues, and in
the same order, in the Epistle to The Colossians (Col. 3:12-13).
Those who are lowly do not offend; those who are meek will not
take offence. They are like Him who was 'meek and lowly in
heart' (Matt. 11:29). Those who suffer long and forbear have the
spirit that will 'outlast pain or provocation',[4] and that is a spirit
which is derived from Christ Himself. All four virtues are motivated and dominated by love; so much so that it is as though he
were to say, Let *love* persuade you to walk in this way. There was
no room in the Greek or Roman world for virtues like these; but
the revelation of God's love in His own dear Son make them
essential for all who would have a character like His.

It was also a vocation to unity; it would call for mutual
fellowship: 'giving diligence to keep the unity of the Spirit in the
bond of peace' (4:3). Holiness of character had an intimate
connection with the fellowship of believers. Paul was indeed very
jealous on this subject. 'Be not unequally yoked with unbeliev-
ers', so he told his converts in the church at Corinth; 'for what
fellowship have righteousness and iniquity?' (2 Cor. 6:14).
Therefore they were to *give diligence*, spare no effort, to uphold
this ideal. Men of holy heart and life would meet each other on
the ground of their faith in Christ, and would enter into that
oneness of spirit which marks fellow members in the household
of God. But this is much more than oneness in the realm of our
own human spirit; it is even more than identity of feeling and
purpose 'generated by a common experience' of God's grace and
mercy.[5] Paul spoke of a *unity* which must trace its origin to the
indwelling of God's Holy Spirit in the body of Christ, and this
indwelling must be realised in the life of every member of that
body. This represents *the unity of the Spirit*, a oneness and identity
of which He is both the secret and the author. This is something
sacred; it ought to be kept, or guarded, with diligence and
vigilance. It is something which will always disclose itself in the

[4] H. C. G. Moule, *ibid*. p. 176.
[5] H. C. G. Moule, *ibid*. p. 177.

mutual relations of one with the other, for it is forged as it were *in the bond of peace*. Paul would use a similar metaphor when he spoke of love 'which is the bond of perfectness' (Col. 3:14). Just as the four virtues were all controlled by the end phrase *in love* (4:2), so this unity, or this fellowship, of the Spirit was now defined in terms of that bond which is *peace*.

No one knew better than Paul the endless variety of racial and religious factors in the background of his readers; but the spiritual realities which they shared would transcend all these lesser differences: 'There is one body, and one Spirit, even as also ye were called in one hope of your calling; one Lord, one faith, one baptism; one God and Father of all, who is over all, and through all, and in all' (4:4-6). This is a grand declaration of the nature and grounds of the mystical unity of which he had spoken. The words read as though they were the fragment of a creed or a hymn which might have been in use among early converts. Seven times in all it reiterates the key word *one*; and that oneness is seen as fact rather than as ideal; and the emphasis rests on the fact that this unity is rooted and grounded in the Triune Godhead. *The unity of the Spirit* is seen in the church as the *one body*, all whose members have been called in *one hope* as they look to the end of their calling. This unity is centralised in *one Lord*, even Jesus, the Son of God, who was received in faith and then confessed in baptism. And this unity climbs to its full splendour in the majesty of God, the *one . . . Father*, who is *over* all, and *through* all, and *in* all. 'Where can such depth and breadth of unity be found as in the fellowship of those who share this faith and experience?'[6] Many attempts would be made from within or from without to disrupt or destroy the mould of that glorious vocation to personal holiness and essential unity. Paul was only the more eager to fix their sight on things that are above and he made this moving appeal for them so to live, to walk so as to please God, that His honour would be upheld.

[6] Francis Foulkes: *The Epistle to The Ephesians (Tyndale N.T. Commentaries)* p. 113.

Chapter Eighteen

The One Divine Pattern of Love

'Husbands, love your wives, even as Christ also loved the
church, and gave himself up for it'.

EPHESIANS 5:25-27

THIS TEXT is a perfect illustration of the incidental statement
of a great truth; it was indeed like Paul's method elsewhere
when he chose to enforce a plain rule of conduct by an appeal
to the highest doctrine (cf. 2 Cor. 8:9; Phil. 2:5). The whole
passage deals with the home circle as the central unit in a stable
society. All that is true and tender in human love is to be
inspired by all that is divine. This was at the heart of the Lord's
saying on the eve of His death: 'A new commandment I give
unto you, that ye love one another; even as I have loved you,
that ye also love one another' (John 13:34; 15:12). This is
more relevant in the sphere of family relations than in any
other social context. Marriage itself is raised to its highest
ideal by the analogy of a divine union between Christ and the
Church: just as husband and wife become one flesh so that they
are no more seen as twain but as one, so he that is joined to the
Lord is one spirit. The whole passage flows out of Paul's
exhortation: 'Be filled with the Spirit . . . subjecting yourselves
one to another in the fear of Christ' (5:18-21). There is no verb
in the next verse, and its structure depends on the participle
subjecting in the verse before. He spoke briefly of wives who
ought to be subject to their husbands: 'for the husband is the
head of the wife, even as Christ also is the head of the church'
(5:23). Then he spoke of husbands for whom the true standard
is the love of Christ in holiness and dignity and self-sacrifice:
they ought to love their wives 'even as Christ also loved the

church and gave himself up for it' (5:25). This truth is then woven into the whole fabric of this passage in such detail that we may turn to it for its doctrine of Christ and the Church as much as for its teaching about husbands and wives.

It is in this Letter that the richest teaching in the New Testament about the Church is found. In this passage, the Church is seen as the Bride and Christ as the Bridegroom in a union that links earth with heaven. This was not a novel image; it was rooted in the language of the Psalms and prophets, and was borrowed by Paul direct from the idea of the Bridal between God and Israel. Ezekiel long before had described how the Lord passed by and beheld Israel: 'Behold, thy time was the time of love; and . . . I sware unto thee, and entered into a covenant with thee, and thou becamest mine' (Ezek. 16:8). Hosea employed the same image with a special vividness: 'I will betroth thee unto me for ever; yea, I will betroth thee unto me in righteousness, and in judgment, and in loving kindness, and in mercies' (Hos. 2:19). Isaiah carried it one step further: 'Thy Maker is thine husband; the Lord of hosts is his name: and the Holy One of Israel is thy redeemer; the God of the whole earth shall he be called' (Isa. 54:5). The Song of Solomon was intended to lift our eyes from an earthly union to its heavenly counterpart with its central message of possession and surrender: 'My beloved is mine, and I am his' (Song of Sol. 2:16; 6:3; 7:10). The New Testament perseveres with this imagery. John the Baptist came as the friend of the Bridegroom, and rejoiced at the Bridegroom's voice (John 3:29). John the Divine saw the consummation of God's purpose for His people as the marriage of the Lamb and His Bride (Rev. 19:7). Thus the Scriptures saw an earthly union as the image of a spiritual, and they pictured the Son of God as One who came to seek a bride on earth. His love for that bride was expressed with an exceeding tenderness by the prophet Jeremiah: 'I have loved thee with an everlasting love: therefore with loving kindness have I drawn thee' (Jer. 31:3).

Paul's use of this imagery was less poetical than that of the prophets, and he began with the practical injunction for a man to love his wife with a love like that of Christ for the church: 'Husbands, love your wives, even as Christ also loved the church, and gave himself up for it' (5:25). Such love is not a thing of time; it belongs neither to today nor to yesterday: it was born in the heart of the Eternal long before time itself began. Husbands, like wives, are the creatures of time, but the standard for their love is nothing less than the self-giving and devotion of Christ Himself. 'Herein is love, not that we loved God, but that he loved us; and sent his Son', in spite of all, 'to be the propitiation for our sins' (1 John 4:10). God so loved the world that He gave His Son; Christ so loved the church that He gave Himself. It makes up a superb double picture: God giving, not sparing, sending His own dear Son; that Son loving, serving, dying to save His people from their sins. Elsewhere Paul had expressed the same thought but in more personal or intimate terms: 'The Son of God loved *me*, and gave himself up for *me*' (Gal. 2:20). He had also told his readers: 'Christ loved *you*, and gave himself up for *you*' (Eph. 5:2 R.V.M.). But here his eyes were not on one person or one group of people; they were on the whole church of God; and if we would know the length and depth and height and breadth of His love towards the church, we must measure it in terms of His suffering and sacrifice on Calvary. Mrs Alexander's famous hymn has expressed it with the utmost simplicity:

We may not know, we can not tell, *what* pains He had to bear,
But we believe it was for us He hung and suffered *there*.

The great object of His love for the church is then set out in a striking sentence: 'that he might sanctify it, having cleansed it by the washing of water with the word' (5:26). This is reminiscent of his address to the church at Corinth in which there were some who had been defiled: 'But ye were washed, but ye were sanctified, . . . in the name of the Lord Jesus Christ, and in the Spirit of our God' (1 Cor. 6:11). There are two verbs in this statement in the Ephesian Epistle: to sanctify and cleanse; and they describe the two aspects of a single experience. God's plan is to sanctify, or to separate, His people for Himself; for this purpose, He has cleansed them from all that would defile. He had chosen a bride for His Son long before the world was made; therefore it was part of His plan that 'we should be holy and without blemish before him in love' (Eph. 1:4). We should be a cleansed and separated people, prepared for His coming, as a bride for that of her bridegroom. The text further suggests that this is to take place by a combination of Sacrament and Evangel; *the washing of water* must be linked with *the word*. There is only one verse in the Pauline Letters which can be seen as a parallel utterance and it is set in a wider context: 'When the kindness of God our Saviour, and his love toward man, appeared, not by works done in righteousness which we did ourselves, but according to his mercy he saved us, through the washing of regeneration and renewing of the Holy Ghost' (Titus 3:4-5). 'The washing of water' and 'the washing of regeneration' seem to refer to the rite of baptism. But it did not stand alone; there was also the ministry of 'the word' and the 'renewing of the Holy Ghost'. So the Son of God gave Himself for the church that He might hallow her like a bride for her union with God.

Such love looks right on to eternity for its ultimate fruition: 'that he might present the church to himself a glorious church, not having spot or wrinkle or any such thing; but that it should be holy and without blemish' (5:27). The same thought was expressed in his declaration to the church at Corinth: 'I espoused you to one husband, that I might present you as a pure virgin to Christ' (2 Cor. 11:2). The royal Bridegroom will bring the church home in all her beauty 'as a bride adorned for her husband' (Rev. 21:2). She will be like the king's daughter, 'all glorious within', fair and lovely in 'garments of wrought gold' (Ps. 45:13). 'Thou art all fair, my love', so He will say; 'there is no spot in thee' (Song of Sol. 4:7). Spots stand for the stains of sin, and wrinkles for the onset of age; but there will be neither spot, nor wrinkle, nor *any such thing*. He will present her in the perfection of beauty and in the plenitude of blessing, both *holy, and without blemish*. This was her predestined character (cf. 1:4); it will be her ultimate attainment (cf. Jude

24). The short Letter from Jude contains one verse in the form of benediction which has more than a mild echo of this Pauline statement: 'Now unto him that is able to guard you from stumbling, and to set you before the presence of his glory without blemish in exceeding joy . . . be glory, majesty, dominion and power before all time, and now, and for evermore' (Jude 24, 25). The Son of God had so set His heart on winning that bride that He had poured out His soul to the point of death; and it was not in vain. He found her when she was defiled, and He cleansed her; He found her when she was far off, and He set her apart for God; He found her while she was naked, and He clothed her in raiment of glory. Such is His love for the church which He has purchased with His own blood (Acts 20:28).

And that is God's standard for us: 'So ought men to love their wives' (5:28 A.V.). Marriage should involve the mutual surrender of each to the other for the Lord's sake, but this must never be at the expense of the primary loyalty of both to Him. Cromwell loved his daughters dearly, as his letters reveal. When his third child, Bridget, was married shortly before her twenty-second birthday, he wrote to her on October 25th, 1646: 'To be a seeker is to be of the best sect next to a finder; and such an one shall every faithful humble seeker be at the end . . . Dear Heart, press on; let not Husband, let not anything cool thy affections after Christ'.[1] Marriage is one beneficent institution which has come down to us from Eden. It was ordained by God Himself at the dawn of human history so that mankind might be increased and children be virtuously brought up in the fear and nurture of God. It was designed because God saw that it was not good for man to dwell alone; he needs to live in fellowship with another as partner and equal. Marriage ought to mean the joy of going through life hand-in-hand with the one of our own choice, sharing one another's burdens, stimulating one another's faith, doubling one another's courage, wearing one another's laurels, and easing

---

[1] Thomas Carlyle, *ibid*. Vol. I, Letter XLI, p. 230.

one another's pain.[2] There is a Psalm whose words will match all who come to marry in that spirit: 'Let the heart of them rejoice that seek the Lord' (Ps. 105:3). Those who rejoice in each other will find that all their joy becomes richer and more complete when they first seek the Lord. This should teach us to put husband or wife before our own self-interest, and to put the Lord Christ first and foremost of all. For how should a man love his wife? And how should a woman love her husband? 'Even as Christ also loved the church, and gave himself up for it'.

[2] cf. M. A. Warren: *Crowded Canvas* p. 45.

Chapter Nineteen

The Whole Armour of God

'Finally, be strong in the Lord, and in the strength of his might'.

EPHESIANS 6:10-13

THERE IS a marked pause at the end of the long and salutary passage on home relationships; then Paul called on his scribe once more and the Letter was brought to a close with a call to arms. He knew that, just like the ancient Spartans, we were born for battle: therefore we must learn to 'endure hardness' as good soldiers of Christ (2 Tim. 2:3 A.V.). We have to live on ground where we will be under attack; it is like a camp in hostile country which must be held until the Captain returns in triumph. Attacks are launched against it by unseen adversaries, for the devil is in command of a vast host. He is always a most aggressive enemy, and that host is skilfully organised for war without quarter. No true soldier of Christ will be immune from its assaults, nor can he be neutral in that conflict. The battlefield is overhung with clouds, and he will be forced to engage in hand-to-hand combat. But each member of that beleagured garrison can stand fast and prevail, because there are sources of strength available in Christ which can make them invincible. Therefore they are to arm themselves from head to foot against the wiles of that foe whose only object is to hurt and destroy. They need the whole glorious panoply of God so that they can stand firm in each crisis, and that divine armour is described in detail. They are to gird themselves with truth and to wear the cuirass of right; they are to put on the sandals of peace and strength, and to grasp their shield with the arm of faith so as to ward off the flaming arrows from the enemy ranks; they are to take God's great mercy as their helmet and His

Word as the sword wrought out on the Spirit's anvil. And they are to let prayer in the widest variety of its practice be their form of vigilant drill and exercise.

The whole passage began with an exhortation to seek a strength that is invincible: 'Finally, be strong in the Lord, and in the strength of his might' (6:10). Paul could draw on his own experience when he wrote in this strain, for he had known what it is to falter. There had been times when he felt so weak in himself that he wondered if he could see things through. But he had found the grace that was equal to all his need (2 Cor. 12:9), and he was strong for all things in Him who never ceased to make him able (Phil. 4:13). This had been the background for his intercession on their behalf: 'That he would grant you . . . that ye may be strengthened with power through his Spirit in the inward man' (3:16). The main phrase is rendered by Moule: 'to be with power made mighty'.[1] Now Paul renewed the same thought in the form of this exhortation: *be strong*; seek strength; strengthen yourselves (cf. 2 Tim. 2:1). This strength did not lie in themselves, but *in the Lord* as the mighty Saviour. To be 'strengthened . . . through his Spirit' (3:16) is now explained; it is to be *strong in the Lord*. This is further defined as *the strength of His might*, and it may be compared with the Colossian reference to being 'strengthened with all power' (Col. 1:11). The phrase is a Hebraic construction; it means *His mighty strength*, a strength put forth in the resurrection of Christ (cf. 1:19). It is where men are that matters; Paul would have them to be *in the Lord* as in an impregnable fortress. Where is the Lord? 'Far above all rule, and authority, and power, and dominion, and every name that is named' (1:21). Where should they be? Seated together 'in Christ Jesus' at God's right hand in the heavenlies (2:6).

They might ask how they should strengthen themselves and the answer was set out in figurative language: 'Put on the whole armour of God, that ye may be able to stand against the wiles of the devil' (6:11). Paul borrowed this imagery from his circumstances at that very moment. He was in chains, handcuffed to a Roman soldier, and he had the time to study each piece of the

---

[1] H. C. G. Moule: *Ephesian Studies* p. 129.

armour worn by his guard. Armour was designed to protect the man; no part of the body should be exposed; the least chink would make him vulnerable. Therefore Paul summoned his readers to gird on the armour which God supplies; *the whole armour*, from head to foot, would be required for this conflict. It was not for them to choose what they liked; they were to put it on entire. He that made it made it for them; He would adapt it so that it would suit the nature and necessity of each. It was not for dress or parade; it was meant for wear in battle. It was only in such armour that they would be *able to stand*. This call *to stand* is the key-note of this passage; three times it rings out its summons (6:11, 13, 14). It is not a summons to men on the march or in an assault; it is a stern command for those who are holding the City of Mansoul. They might be forced to stand with their backs to the wall, but at all costs they were to stand their ground *against the wiles of the devil* (cf. 4:14). They were aware that his attacks were marked by shift and stealth, by subtlety and stratagem, at times when men were off their guard. Therefore they could not stand at ease; they were to stand as men who were armed and alert against all 'the wiles of error' (4:14). And so standing, they had nothing to fear; the Lord would put forth all His strength on their behalf.

Human strength may suffice in a human conflict, but it is no match for spiritual warfare: 'For our wrestling is not against flesh and blood, but against the principalities, against the powers, against the world-rulers of this darkness, against the spiritual hosts of wickedness in the heavenly places' (6:12). The phrase *flesh and blood* is used to denote ordinary men and women (cf. 1 Cor. 15:50; Gal. 1:16), and it is in contrast with the far more dangerous enemies who are found in the unseen world of spirits. There was no doubt in Paul's mind as to the objective existence of such evil spirits, and he listed some of them as agents of the master mind in that world of wickedness. His catalogue of synonyms for the hosts of evil may be compared with the similar catalogue for the angels of light (1:21; cf. 3:10), and the emphatic recurrence of the preposition before each noun suggests that each is to be seen as a separate enemy. *Principalities* and *powers* were terms which he had used elsewhere to sum up the leaders of all organised rebellion against the throne of God (cf. Rom. 8:38; Col. 2:15). *The world-rulers of this darkness* are those who hold mysterious empire over this world in its aspect as the scene of evil (cf. Col. 1:13). The world is in darkness because it is the realm where the devil holds sway (cf. Luke 22:53); it is darkened by the shadows of guilt and pain and death. *The spiritual hosts of wickedness* are the invisible agents of all that is wicked, and they are even in *the heavenly places*. This is the seventh and last occasion for the use of this word, and the only case in which it is linked with evil. Heaven is seen as in antithesis to earth, and the hosts of evil spirits hover like birds of prey over 'the landscape of humanity'.[2]

This grim and quite frightening description of the spiritual forces all drawn up in hostile array constrained Paul to reiterate the stern summons to arm for the hour of battle: 'Wherefore take up the whole armour of God, that ye may be able to withstand in the evil day, and having done all, to stand' (6:13). There is a change from the command to *put on* (6:11); this fresh call is to *take up*. The two must be combined in order to complete the full picture. H. C. G. Moule compared it with Aeneas who took up and put on the whole warrior panoply on the verge of battle.[3] There is a sense of fresh and vigorous emphasis in the call for nothing less than *the whole armour of God* before he began to describe it in detail. He spoke of this and that as meant for their defence against the foe; but in essence, each piece must be interpreted in terms of Christ Himself. *The whole armour of God* is Christ, or else is found in Christ, and this command has its obvious counterpart in the summons elsewhere to *put on the Lord Jesus Christ* (Rom. 13:14). It is only as men are clothed in Christ that they will be *able to withstand*. This word is a compound form of the verb *to stand*, and its purpose is to denote a stand in the face of intense opposition (cf. Jas. 4:7; 1 Pet. 5:9). Such a stand will be most needed *in the evil day*, the day of trial or persecution, when the conflict is most severe (cf. 5:16). It does not point to one solitary crisis; it is any crisis which may arise in this continuing struggle. They were called to be in this fight to the very

[2] H. C. G. Moule: *Ephesian Studies*, 1898, p. 325.
[3] H. C. G. Moule, *ibid*. pp. 327–328, footnote 2.

finish; therefore, *having done all*, having put forth all their effort, they were *to stand*. They were to hold their ground as men who knew what it was to be fixed, steadfast, 'unmoveable' (1 Cor. 15:58), ready for fresh assaults.

Paul went on to describe each piece of this armour in a series of short vivid figures of speech. Six pieces were mentioned with some spiritual application (6:14-17), and the soldier so armed was then summoned to keep his watch in prayer (6:18). Then with lightning quickness he moved from the field of conflict and the armour of God for each particular convert to all the saints and to himself (6:18-20). He gave up the figurative language of word pictures for an appeal that was intensely personal. The whole armour of God was a magnificent concept, and Paul employed it with perfect élan. But the spiritual realities which lie behind each fresh picture must be allowed to shine through our understanding. The Person and office of Christ stands as it were behind each piece of this armour, and he would have them learn how to use Christ in faith if they were to ward off the powers of darkness. There was nothing in this list of arms to protect the back; they were to stand with their face to the foe. What would be thought of a soldier who went into battle without his arms or who fell asleep on his watch? There is never a time when the Christian warrior does not need to lay hold on Christ and to rely on Him to bear the brunt of each assault. 'He that believeth on him shall not be put to shame' (1 Pet. 2:6). And Paul himself was to exemplify all that he taught. He was in the front of that field; he stood his ground in the time of battle; and when he had fought to the end, he came as a victor from the conflict (2 Tim. 4:7-8).

I bless Thee for the quiet rest Thy servant taketh now;
I bless Thee for his blessedness, and for his crownèd brow:
For every weary step he trod in faithful following Thee,
And for the good fight foughten well, and closed right
    valiantly.[4]

---

[4] Mrs A. Stuart-Menteith: *Lays of the Kirk and Covenant*.

Chapter Twenty

The Hope of Glory

'Christ in you, the hope of glory'.

COLOSSIANS 1:25-27

THE FIRST chapter in the Epistle to the Colossians is rich in the magnificent Christology of its central passage. This was rounded off at length with a firm application to Paul's Gentile converts in the Valley of the Lycus: 'And you . . . hath he reconciled in the body of his flesh through death, to present you holy and without blemish and unreproveable before him: if so be that ye continue in the faith, grounded and stedfast, and not moved away from the hope of the Gospel' (1:21-23). This led to a personal reference in his customary manner which he could not resist: 'whereof I Paul was made a minister' (1:23). That in turn led to a further interruption in the main line of thought while he glanced at the sufferings which he had been called to endure. Then he resumed what he had been saying with the same phrase: 'Whereof I was made a minister, according to the dispensation of God which was given me to you-ward, to fulfil the word of God' (1:25). His words equate 'the hope of the Gospel' (1:23) with 'the word of God' (1:25), and this is explained as 'the mystery which hath been hid from all ages and generations: but now hath it been manifested to his saints' (1:26). The word *mystery* is a technical term with its own distinct meaning; this has nothing to do with its use in modern English. It was used of something which could only become known by revelation; it is like a divine secret which God has been pleased to disclose in the fulness of time. It was hidden; now it has been revealed. It is found six times in Ephesians and four times in Colossians, and all except one case

115

(Eph. 5:32) refer to the fact that in Christ, Gentiles are as welcome in the kingdom of God as Jews.

But this doctrine was so revolutionary that Paul felt bound to speak further so as to bring out its astonishing implications: 'To whom God was pleased to make known what is the riches of the glory of this mystery among the Gentiles' (1:27). It may be hard for the modern reader to grasp what this amazing *mystery* meant for a man like Paul. The Jews could not conceive that there might be a place for the Gentiles in God's kingdom unless they were ready to be identified with the Jewish nation by the rite of circumcision. The Jews saw the Gentiles as those who were strangers to the covenants and the promises of God; they were aliens, enemies, 'far off', without hope in this world or in the world to come (Eph. 2:12, 13). It was the same whether they were Greek or Roman, barbarian or Scythian; it was a stark racial attitude which is perfectly reflected in the words of Rudyard Kipling about 'the lesser breeds without the law'. This had been as deeply ingrained in the mind of Saul of Tarsus as anything else in the traditions of his fathers (Gal. 1:14); it had required nothing less than a clear revelation from God to change his mind. But it had pleased God to reveal His Son in him so that he might preach Him among the Gentiles (Gal. 1:16). As a result, he had learnt to describe himself as the apostle of the uncircumcised; he saw this as his own unique calling, and he had won recognition for it from those who were pillars in the church at Jerusalem (Gal. 2:9). Nevertheless he was at heart far more Jewish than he could see; he could never shake off his own essential Jewishness. He may have been hardly aware of it, but his Gentile converts were not likely to miss the fact. It came out plain and clear in the way in which he spoke of *this mystery* among the Gentiles.

Paul's next words went to the very heart of this mystery and interpret it in ever memorable language: 'which is Christ in you, the hope of glory' (1:27). He had never lost his sense of wonder at God's mercy for those who were Gentiles. This was something which seemed to need explanation in his eyes much more than it did in theirs. Amazed as he always was that God had chosen a Jew such as he had once been, he was far more amazed that He should choose Gentiles on the same terms. This was one great reason why the doctrines of grace, God's most gracious favour, without regard to creed or race, formed the bed-rock basis of his proclamation of the Gospel. But he went on in this passage to unfold and explain the riches and glory of that open secret, and his sense of wonder breaks through in an astonishing parenthesis. What was that *mystery?* What was that truth, hidden for so many generations but now at last revealed? It was nothing less than 'Christ in you, the hope of glory'. It was not the bare fact of *Christ* alone, though the hope of all the ages had been summed up in Him. It was the fact that this Christ was in them, just as He was in those who were Hebrew converts; and that was true, Gentile though they were and pagans as they had been. The man who is *in* Christ soon finds that this Christ is *in* him. It is just as hard or just as simple to grasp the one as it is the other. It is picture language; but no other language will so clearly convey the truth. Paul's three words, *Christ in you*, point to nothing less than the full personal indwelling of Christ in the very spirit of His own words: 'ye in me, and I in you' (John 14:20).

Many words of Scripture present the Lord Christ to us as in the truest nearness, but this union is such that the word *in* must be used to convey its full meaning: 'Christ *in* you'. The risen Lord Jesus had given a special promise to His disciples: 'Lo, I am *with* you alway, even unto the end of the world' (Matt. 28:20). But Paul's words go beyond that great promise in their statement of a yet more intimate connection. Christ, the image of the invisible God, the First-born of the created universe, and the Head of the church: this Christ is now *in* you as those who are sons and daughters of God. He is *in* you as the One whose presence within spells a valid title to the hope of glory. This is the root meaning of his challenge to the church at Corinth: 'Try your own selves, whether ye be in the faith; prove your own selves. Or know ye not as to your own selves, that Jesus Christ is *in* you?' (2 Cor. 13:5). He is *in* you as the One whose Spirit will create a moral fitness for the hope of glory. This was at the bottom of his yearning utterance for the Galatians: 'My little children, of whom I am again in travail until Christ be formed *in* you' (Gal. 4:19). This is the Christ who will come *in* if any man opens the door (Rev. 3:20), and who will live *in* me if I have been nailed to the cross with Him (Gal. 2:20). The full development of all that this phrase means may be found in the prayer for his converts: 'that Christ may dwell *in your hearts* through faith' (Eph. 3:17). This does not mean that there is some kind of heavenly influence that lives on in our lives; nor does it mean that this presence within is no more than some vague kind of spiritual experience. It is the Lord Himself who is resident in our hearts, and the word *in* points to a total saving union of the living Christ with each truly believing man or woman whether Jew or Gentile.

It would have been enough if Paul had been content to interpret the mystery as *Christ in you*; but he chose to expand the phrase with the further statement that it is Christ in you who is *the hope of glory* (1:27). Paul had spoken about 'the *hope* of the Gospel' in his initial reference to their need for continuance in a steadfast spirit (1:23). Peter spoke of 'the *hope* that is in you' in his exhortation to the believer to be ready to furnish a reasonable answer to an honest question (1 Pet. 3:15). What is that hope? It is nothing other than Christ Himself, received by faith to dwell within and then obeyed as Lord of all. This Christ who was *for* you on the cross and is *in* you as the Lord is *the hope of glory*. This was in strong contrast with their lot by nature, and he addressed them as Gentiles: 'Ye were at that time separate from Christ, . . . having *no hope* and without God in the world' (Eph. 2:12). But God plans to call His people out of every tribe and nation; His grace reaches out to Gentiles just as it does to Jews. There is only one remedy or provision, and it is the same for all men. Those who were once far off are made nigh in the blood of Christ (Eph. 2:13); and the benefits of that so great salvation mean that He dwells in their hearts through faith and prepares them so that they will share in His glory. This is not just a vague ideal, far off, remote, and out of reach; it is even now a vital reality because the Christ within is the hope of glory. That is not a height to scale, but a rock on which to stand; not something to attain, but a fact to accept. It was impossible for Paul to state strongly enough that the presence of Christ within as the hope of glory is a sober fact for faith and joyful recognition.

The most attractive reference to *hope* in the Pauline writings is found in his words of benediction for the Thessalonian converts: 'Now our Lord Jesus Christ himself, and God our Father which loved us and gave us *eternal hope through grace*, comfort your hearts and stablish them in every good work and word' (2 Thess. 2:16-17). This was *the hope* which shed its light on the darkest days of persecution. This is why it has been cherished by men of God all down the stream of time. Jacob had to lean on his staff to the end of his life because of the sinew that shrank when he wrestled all night with the angel of God; but he had a better stay for his soul. He paused in the midst of blessing his sons and voiced the hope of a glorious certainty: 'I have waited for thy salvation, O Lord' (Gen. 49:18). It was as though he were to say: 'I have waited, and now it is mine'. Simeon with the Christ-child in his arms was content for his life to move to its close: 'For mine eyes have seen thy salvation which thou hast prepared before the face of all people' (Luke 2:32). John Charles Ryle has drawn the contrast between those who have a sure hope and those who have none at all. 'When Cardinal Beaufort lay on his death-bed, Shakespeare described King Henry as saying, 'He dies, but gives no sign!' When John Knox was near his end and unable to speak, he was asked to give some proof that the Gospel he had proclaimed in life brought him comfort in death. He heard, and raised his hand three times, and died.[1] John Wesley could affirm: 'Our people die well; the world may find fault with our opinions; but the world can never deny that our people die well'.[2] Let the humblest man or woman only grasp the wonder of the fact that Christ is in him, and he may draw into his soul all the comfort of that hope of glory.

[1] J. C. Ryle: *Practical Religion*, pp. 486–7.
[2] J. C. Ryle: *The Christian Leaders of the Last Century* (1880 edition) p. 173.

Chapter Twenty-one

The Treasures of Wisdom

'In whom are all the treasures of wisdom and knowledge
hidden'.

COLOSSIANS 2:1-3

THE FIRST chapter concludes with a statement about apostolic
testimony: this Christ, the Christ who is in you, we now proclaim
to each and all. Paul was often moved to revert to the theme of his
own calling and his supreme desire to make the Lord Christ
known. It was like the fire that Moses saw in the bush that burned
and yet was not consumed; no man ever saw the ashes of that fire
in Paul's heart once it had been kindled by the flame of God's
love. So he seized the mention of the Christ who is the hope of
glory in order to remind them of his own constant testimony:
'Whom we proclaim, admonishing every man and teaching
every man in all wisdom, that we may present every man perfect
in Christ' (1:28). It was his aim to present his converts as those
who were perfectly instructed and had become spiritually mature
in their knowledge of Christ: 'Whereunto I labour also, striving
according to his working, which worketh in me mightily' (1:29).
The word *labour* was in special use to describe an athlete in
training; it was naturally linked with the word *striving*, agonis-
ing, contending in the arena. The two words are coupled in
another Epistle with striking effect: 'To this end we *labour* and
strive, because we have our hope set on the living God who is the
Saviour of all men, specially of them that believe' (1 Tim. 4:10).
Paul saw himself as so intent on being able to present his readers
as 'perfect in Christ' that he threw himself into the contest with
all the ardour of a totally dedicated athlete. He trained himself,
laboured, in the school of discipline and self-denial; he was willing

to *strive*, to agonise, in the arena even if the utmost effort were to call for suffering as well. And this he sought to do, not in reckless waste, but *in all wisdom*.

There is no break in the line of thought at the end of the chapter; the metaphor was continued as Paul began a new section in the next verse: 'For I would have you know how greatly I strive for you' (2:1). He had already hinted at an *arena* and an *agony* which were involved in his apostolic labours, and he wanted them to understand the real magnitude of that *conflict* (2:1 A.V.). It would include all the turmoil of which he had spoken in his Letter to the Church at Corinth: 'we were afflicted on every side; without were fightings, within were fears' (2. Cor. 7:5). There were chains on his wrists at that very moment, and he was in prison on their behalf. But the inward struggle for their spiritual welfare was the leading idea behind his words, and the form this would take is made clear by reference to the case of Epaphras: 'Epaphras, who is one of you, a servant of Christ Jesus, saluteth you, always *striving* for you in his prayers, that ye may stand perfect and fully assured in all the will of God' (4:12). The one outlet available to Epaphras in his anxiety on their behalf was in the form of prayer. The same outlet was in constant use in Paul's case as well, and his prayers in prison for his far-off converts have a quality that time can not diminish and an appeal that will not die. But there was more than the fervent labour of prayer on their behalf (cf. 4:12 A.V.); he had already suggested something which was much more profound: 'I rejoice in my sufferings for your sake, and fill up on my part that which is lacking of the afflictions of Christ in my flesh for his body's sake, which is the church, whereof I was made a minister' (1:24-25). There are depths in these words which we may not fathom, but they shed some light on *how greatly* he agonised in that conflict on their behalf.

The text as a whole made it clear that his love and concern reached out to the widest circle: 'for you, and for them at Laodicea, and for as many as have not seen my face in the flesh' (2:1). There were three small townships in the Valley of the Lycus about one hundred miles inland from the great maritime and mercantile city of Ephesus. They formed a triangle and had close connections with each other. Hierapolis is the least known and is barely mentioned in the New Testament (Col. 4:13). Colossae has left its name in Christian history through the Pauline Letters and Laodicea through The Revelation of St John the Divine. There were people like Epaphras and Philemon who came from that inland Valley. They had heard and met Paul during his residence in Ephesus and had returned home with a saving knowledge of Christ in their hearts. Epaphras had become the chief evangelist of these three towns (Col. 4:12-13; Philemon 23); Philemon was the convert in whose house the church at Colossae was wont to meet (Philemon 2). Paul had never travelled inland to visit the Valley of the Lycus and the majority of those converts had yet to see him 'in the flesh' (2:1). But he rejoiced at news of the churches which had sprung up and was deeply concerned for their ongoing character in stability and maturity of faith. He could hardly fail to know that Colossae was exposed to the subtle force of Gnostic teaching or that Laodicea was always in danger of growing mean and lukewarm. The care of all the churches had been laid on his shoulders; converts like these whom he had not seen, as well as others. He was constrained by that sense of care to pour out his heart for them whether in prayer or in appeal in a spirit of agony and urgency.

No one could have been more tender or more anxious for their spiritual welfare; not Epaphras; not Philemon: 'that their hearts may be comforted, being knit together in love' (2:2). It was as though they would meet heart to heart, even though they could not meet face to face. It is reminiscent of a much more personal nostalgic message to his Thessalonian converts: 'But we, brethren, being bereaved of you for a short season, *in presence, not in heart*, endeavoured the more exceedingly *to see your face* with great desire' (1 Thess. 2:17). The word *comforted* is used in its older meaning and in modern English would be better rendered *encouraged*. He longed to know that they drew strength into their souls in true Christian fellowship, for this would mean that they were *knit together*, united, compacted, like limbs in one body (cf. Eph. 4:16). Such a relationship would need the kind of bond that love imparts; it would only become significant in their experience if it were in fact sealed *in love*. This was something radically new in Gentile society in east and west alike; it lay outside the experience or comprehension of those who had grown up in the customs of idol worship and pagan culture. But Paul was well aware of the astonishing reality of love as the secret of true Christian fellowship. This was love in the rich sense of that term which had come into use as a direct result of the revelation of the supreme self-giving love of God in Jesus Christ. They were to love each other as He had loved them; and they could not do this unless they first drank for themselves from the well of His great love for them. The expression of unity *in love* would be the mark of a healthy congregation; they could not flourish without it.

This travail in spirit on their behalf reached out for a happy issue in the future: 'unto all riches of the full assurance of understanding, that they may know the mystery of God, even Christ' (2:2). A note in the Revised Version declares that 'the ancient authorities vary much in the text of this passage'. The New International Version brings out the force of the preposition which was used in each clause in the Greek text: '*so that* they may have the full riches of complete understanding, *in order that* they may know the mystery of God, namely, Christ'. The image of *riches* in spiritual matters was frequent in Paul's prison letters, and here it is applied to their growth in 'assured understanding' (R.S.V.). He spoke of this in the context of fellowship and unity which were rooted in love, and he longed for them to enter into all the wealth of mature insight and settled conviction. This was in sharp contrast with the indecision of the speculative philosophy of an incipient Gnosticism: that could only impoverish and would end in spiritual destitution. Those who have an *assured understanding* owe it all to the grace of God, and ought to grow in its strength and comfort. Mental capacity will be enlarged; spiritual insight will be enriched; for there is no limit to the riches which have become accessible for those in whose heart the Lord Christ has come to dwell. But the sentence does not end at that point; what was the goal Paul had in view? It was all in order that they might know *the mystery of God*; that is, that those who were Gentiles might share in the knowledge of that divine secret. That *mystery* now lies open; the long preserved secret has been revealed; it is *even Christ*, that same Christ who is *in you* (1:27).

The bare mention of Christ was then amplified in words of great dignity: 'In whom are all the treasures of wisdom and knowledge hidden' (2:3). The image of riches was thus carried further, and the riches were pictured as treasures hidden in a mine which can be explored. But the treasures were then defined as *wisdom* and *knowledge*. These two words were coupled else-where, and in the same order. Paul had spoken of 'the riches both of the wisdom and the knowledge of God' (Rom. 11:33). He had taken pains to treat them as two separate elements: 'For to one is given through the Spirit the word of wisdom; and to another the word of knowledge, according to the same Spirit' (1 Cor. 12:8). The Greeks set their hearts on wisdom as the ideal attainment; but they did not know 'the fear of the Lord' which is 'the beginning of wisdom' (Prov. 9:10). Gnostics thought that knowledge was the supreme ideal, but they did not know Him whom to know is life eternal (John 17:3). Wisdom refers to spiritual insight; knowledge refers to spiritual understanding; and they are both essential elements for maturity and stability. Wisdom will convey the ideas of perception and discernment; it will teach men how to judge or how to decide aright. Knowledge will convey the idea of strong mental grasp of the truth; it will lead men to know God in the fulness of His self-disclosure. Such gifts will bring richer knowledge of God and better understand-ing of men; and they are all hidden in Christ for His people to explore and possess. These riches of wisdom and treasures of knowledge may all be found in Him; and that is the final answer to Greek and Gnostic alike in all that concerns those who would be 'perfect in Christ' (1:28).

Chapter Twenty-two

His Peace and His Word

'Let the peace of Christ rule in your hearts. . . . Let the
word of Christ dwell in you richly'.
                              COLOSSIANS 3: 15-16

PAUL HAD spoken of the need to put on the new clothes of the
new man; that is, 'a heart of compassion, kindness, humility,
meekness, long-suffering' (3:12). These were essentially Christ-
like virtues; they would not be highly esteemed in the pagan
environment of the Valley of the Lycus. They were the marks
of Christ Himself, and the same marks should be found in the
lives of those who bear His Name. The list runs on; the
forbearance and forgiveness which He displayed were named.
Above all, there was love as the supreme virtue and the bond
of perfect harmony. Then two verses follow which set out in
plain terms the most practical injunction for a godly manner
of life: 'And let the peace of Christ rule in your hearts, to the
which also ye were called in one body; and be ye thankful. Let
the word of Christ dwell in you richly in all wisdom; teaching
and admonishing one another with psalms and hymns and
spiritual songs, singing with grace in your hearts unto God'
(3:15-16). The main theme in these two verses is *the peace of
Christ* and *the Word of Christ*; but neither is treated as it were
in isolation. They are both set in the context of the social
virtues; each is shown to have a special outlet. His peace flows
out in a thankful spirit: *be ye thankful*. This was indeed a key
message in this Letter; it is mentioned in each of the four short
chapters (1:3; 2:7; 3:15; 4:2). His Word issues in songs of
praise: *singing with grace in your hearts*. This was itself a fine
testimony to the practice of the earliest disciples; it is a clear

125

echo of his language in a companion Epistle (Eph. 5:19). There is music in the text as a whole and this makes it linger in heart and mind; for to experience His peace we must learn to absorb His word.

The first theme was that of His peace and its issue in a thankful spirit: 'And let the peace of Christ rule in your hearts, to the which also ye were called in one body; and be ye thankful' (3:15). We are in need of the arbitration of peace for the sake of poise and maturity; the peace that ruled the heart of Christ must rule our hearts likewise. His was the most poised and balanced life this world has yet seen and the secret was the peace which held His heart in control. He was never wrongly provoked, never caught off balance, nor out of step, nor ill at ease, because the peace of God was a strong and vibrant reality in His experience. It was this peace which He left as His one legacy for the disciples: 'Peace I leave with you; *My peace* I give unto you' (John 14:27). This was not only peace with God as the result of forgiveness; it was also the peace of God as the secret of fellowship. 'These things have I spoken unto you', He said, 'that *in Me* ye may have peace' (John 16:33). In the world, they would have tribulation; in Him, they would have peace. This was endorsed by His double salutation when He appeared to them on the evening of the day of resurrection: 'Jesus came and stood in the midst, and saith unto them, Peace be unto you' (John 20:19, 21). So then Paul would argue, where the world speaks of poise, let this peace rule within our hearts. The verb *to rule* refers to the man who acted as an umpire in the Greek games; from this it came to mean, first of all, to judge, and then to rule. It is a very telling word-picture when it is applied to the heart, and Paul used it with the insight of true spiritual psychology. Why should the heart be in turmoil? If Christ be in you the hope of glory, then His peace is to referee or arbitrate, and so to rule all that goes on within.

The realm in which this peace is to act is that of the mind and heart (cf. Phil. 4:7), because that is the realm in which conflict and tension will arise. We are inclined to dwell on our perplexities until we do not know how to switch off the current of our thoughts. We get so keyed up with apprehension or with anxiety that our nerves are on edge. Human strain and tension are the cause of ills and troubles for both mind and body in more ways than we can number. What we need — and what words can adequately express it? — is that peace of God which passes understanding (Phil. 4:7). It will mount guard like a sentinel to watch over what is vulnerable in the garrison of heart and mind. It will step in where the strife of inward debate occurs because its role is to judge and prevail. Conflict between self and God, or between self and others, must be subject to that arbitration. Strife of motive, reason, impulse, desire, must be referred to that umpire. Nor is that peace for our own sake alone; it is for the welfare of the whole church. The man who has Christ's own peace in his heart will stand for peace in the larger body. Conflict always results from rivalry and bitterness, contention and resentment; but the reality of His peace in the heart precludes the forces of conflict and strengthens the oneness of the entire body. It will find a proper outlet in a truly thankful spirit. Paul may have had in mind the words of the Psalmist when he drew his picture of the tribes of Israel on their way up to the temple. In what spirit ought they to come before the Lord their God? 'Go your way into his gates with thanksgiving, and into his courts with praise; *be thankful unto Him*, and speak good of his Name'(Ps. 100:3).[1]

The next theme was that of His word and its issue in a joyful spirit: 'Let the word of Christ dwell in you richly in all wisdom; teaching and admonishing one another with psalms and hymns and spiritual songs, singing with grace in your hearts unto God' (3:16). We are in need of the authority of truth for the sake of depth and stability; the Word that filled the mind of Christ must fill our minds likewise. No one who now reads the Gospel records can fail to see that His mind was saturated with the Hebrew Scriptures. He was more at home in the Law and the Prophets than were the scribes themselves. They were masters of its letter, but there was no moral force in the things they had to say; but He spoke with authority because of His

[1] Coverdale's Translation in The Book of Common Prayer, 1662.

spiritual insight into all that the Law and the Prophets represented. This was more than knowledge of the text and content of the Hebrew Scriptures; it indicated an understanding of truth which amazed them all. He was never afraid to take His stand on the ground of what was written or to appeal to its authority as final and supreme. This was made clear by His constant challenge to critics and others: 'Have ye not read?' (Matt. 12:3, 5; 19:4; 21:16, 42; 22:31). But God who spoke to the fathers at sundry times and in divers manners by the prophets spoke at last by His Son; and this revelation is now spoken of as *the Word of Christ*. This points to the message of the Gospel, the good news made articulate by Him, the full revelation of God which He came to make known. There was never any contradiction between His word and the Hebrew Scriptures; He had come to fulfil the Law and the Prophets. But there was no hesitation in His emphatic utterance: 'I say unto you' (Matt. 5:18, 20, 22, 26, 28, 32, 34, 39, 44). This is *the Word of Christ* which stamps itself with His authority upon our minds.

The true nature of the Gospel is marked by its designation as a word or message. This would mean in part the written message of the prophets from which He had expounded the things concerning Himself. It would also mean in part the oral teaching of the Apostles which now exists for us only in the pages of the New Testament. It is above all else *the Word of Christ*, good news which He proclaimed. This Word is to lodge in our minds as a permanent element in our thought and activity. It should dwell there *richly*, pouring itself into the reservoirs of memory; and it should dwell there *in all wisdom*, in all kinds of wisdom (cf. 1:9; Eph. 1:8). This is something far more than the finest tact or largeness of mind; it is infinitely better than to know its *letter* as did the scribes. It is to know its *spirit*, to feel its power, and so to draw on its life-giving properties; then it will pour itself out in psalms and hymns and songs, all sung *with grace* in the heart before the Lord (cf. Eph. 5:19).

When the younger Pliny was Pro-consul of Bithynia shortly

after the start of the second Christian century, he consulted the Emperor Trajan as to how he should deal with those who were professing Christians. He described their customs as far as he had been able to learn the facts; they seemed harmless enough. They used to meet before daylight on a certain day of the week, and then they sang a hymn of praise to Christ as God. This was remarkable testimony from a pagan writer to the effect that they worshipped Christ as God, and that their worship was marked by hymns of praise. And so, across the long ages, through the silence of now forgotten centuries, we may catch the echo of those hymns of praise on the lips of men in whom *the Word of Christ* had lodged *in all wisdom*.

These two verses form a couplet in which Paul set out two brief laws of the spiritual life with pellucid clarity: 'Let the peace of Christ rule in your heart. . . Let the word of Christ dwell in you richly'. The peace of Christ and the word of Christ are like streams that flow in a common channel, and such was the experience of the veteran Puritan, Richard Baxter. His life spanned the troubled reigns of the four Stuart monarchs, and his ministry reached its apex at Kidderminster under the Commonwealth. On the Restoration of Charles II, he was driven from Church and Cure by the Act of Uniformity, and for twenty-five years he was subject to the incessant vexation which had become the lot of the Non-Conformists. He was taxed, fined, and dogged by spies; he was driven from his home and silenced in the pulpit. In his seventieth year, he was dragged before Jeffreys as Chief Justice and was sentenced to an indefinite term in prison. But his faith shone brightest when the night was darkest as his *Poetical Fragments* reveal:

> Now it belongs not to my care,
>   Whether I die or live:
> To love and serve Thee is my share:
>   And this Thy grace must give.[2]

He was released from his imprisonment on the flight of James II from England; but overwhelmed with infirmities and

2 J. T. Wilkinson: *Richard Baxter and Margaret Charlton* p. 177.

penniless from adversities, he had not long to live. His life
began to move gently towards its close in the course of 1691.
Friends came in to see him, and he was heard to murmur: 'I
have pain; there is no arguing against sense. But I have peace;
I have peace'.[3] 'Mark the perfect man, and behold the upright:
for the end of that man is peace' (Ps. 37:37 A.V.).

---

[3] J. M. Lloyd Thomas: *The Autobiography of Richard Baxter*, Appendix 1, p. 266.

Chapter Twenty-three

Prayerful, Watchful, Thankful

'Continue steadfastly in prayer, watching therein with
thanksgiving'.

COLOSSIANS 4:2-6

THE SCOPE of Paul's thought now broadens out from rules of
domestic behaviour and the text turns to the primary requisites
of a true life for God: 'Continue steadfastly in prayer, watching
therein with thanksgiving' (4:2). Continuance in prayer means
to remain constant in the practice of all the elements of real
heart communion with God. The same combination of words
is found in the record of the earliest disciples (Acts 1:14; 2:42;
6:4). It was also used by Paul on another occasion in one of his
staccato expressions: 'continuing steadfastly in prayer' (Rom.
12:12). Such continuance or perseverance in prayer must be
sustained by a spirit of watchfulness and thankfulness. It is
imperative that men should be watchful if their prayers are to
have spiritual vitality. The heart must be awake; the mind
must be alert. It is only when this is so that men engage in
prayer with the disciplined attention of those who know their
God and do exploits. To be watchful is the reverse of the listless
spirit which makes people careless and soon deflects them from
the need to pray altogether. We ought to be watchful in view
of the apathetic spirit in the world all around: 'Watch therefore:
for ye know not on what day your Lord cometh' (Matt. 24:42).
We ought to be watchful in view of the wiles of Satan: 'Watch
and pray, that ye enter not into temptation' (Matt. 26:41).
But the broadest meaning must be attached to the summons
to be watchful in prayer: 'Praying at all seasons . . . and
watching thereunto in all perseverance' (Eph. 6:18). Prayer is

not a luxury or an opiate; true prayer is a strenuous exercise and will demand concentration. The Lord voiced a ringing summons in this spirit: 'What I say unto you I say unto all, Watch' (Mark 13:37).

It is no less imperative that men should be thankful if their prayers are to have spiritual vitality: 'Continue steadfastly in prayer, watching therein with thanksgiving'. A thankful heart is something we all expect in others; we are disappointed when we do not find it (cf. Luke 17:17). This element of thanksgiving should be normal, for the recollection of God's goodness always imparts spiritual freshness to those who pray. And yet this is all too easily forgotten; it is especially hard to give thanks and to rejoice in time of trial. Nevertheless this word and its cognates are so frequent in the Pauline Letters that there is no room for mistake, and the duty of thanksgiving has a special prominence in this Epistle. It is mentioned in one form or other in each consecutive chapter (1:3; 2:7; 3:15; 4:2) just as the note of joy had been sounded in each chapter of the Philippian Letter (1:18; 2:17-18; 3:1; 4:4). Paul taught them how to look up to God in creation, and in providence, and in redemption, knowing that in every sphere they would find fresh and delightful incentives for a thankful spirit. He saw the need for thanksgiving in all circumstances: 'In nothing be anxious; but in everything by prayer and supplication with thanksgiving let your requests be made known unto God' (Phil. 4:6). Are we truly thankful when we are glad? There are subtle shades of meaning which lie behind what it is to be glad and what it is to be thankful. Gladness is the spirit of a child who receives a gift and looks at it with great pleasure; thankfulness is the response of an adult who looks at the giver and loves him all the more. So this call to continuance in prayer demands both patience and purpose in a watchful and a thankful spirit.

Paul's swift sequence of thought travelled on from wider exhortation to a particular request for prayer: 'Withal praying for us also, that God may open unto us a door for the word, to speak the mystery of Christ' (4:3). There were frequent requests in his Letters for such personal remembrance of him on the part of converts (Rom. 15:30; Eph. 6:19; 1 Thess. 3:25; 2 Thess. 3:1). His choice of the plural pronoun in this case shows that he meant to include preachers like Timothy and Epaphras in his request (Col. 1:1; 4:12). He would have them pray with special intent that it might please God to *open . . . a door* for the message of the Gospel. The same attractive metaphor had been employed to describe the favourable circumstances for preaching the Gospel which he had found both in Corinth and in Troas (1 Cor. 16:9; 2 Cor. 2:12). This word-picture of an open door always represents opportunity; in this context, it was opportunity to preach *the word* of grace. This is not the same thought as that in the Ephesian parallel, although it is set in the same context. In that passage, he asked for prayer that his preaching might be full of courage: 'that I may *open my mouth* boldly to make known the mystery of the Gospel' (Eph. 6:19 A.V.). He longed for that open door in order to proclaim *the mystery of Christ*. The word *mystery* was a technical term which he had borrowed from the mystery religions of the eastern Mediterranean, but he gave it a new meaning in the context of a Christian vocabulary. The old ideas of secrecy and conceal-ment vanished, and it came to imply a truth which had remained unknown until it was disclosed by the revelation of God (cf. Eph. 1:9; 3:3; 3:4; 3:9; 5:32; 6:19; Col. 1:26; 1:27; 2:2). It was the great open secret of the Gospel, and its leading idea was that Gentiles were now welcome on the same terms as Jews to the saving grace and goodness of God.

The tone of this passage becomes still more personal as the plural number of the pronoun changes to the singular with a direct reference to his special dilemma: 'for which I am also in bonds; that I may make it manifest, as I ought to speak' (2:3-4). It was because he had refused to insist on Gentile obedience to the law of Moses as a pre-requisite for his Gentile converts that he had been condemned both to imprisonment and bonds. He would in fact have been a free man at that very moment if he had not put the need of the Gentiles before his own freedom. He had mentioned his bonds in the same way in the companion Epistle: 'For which I am an ambassador in chains; that in it I may speak boldly, as I ought to speak' (Eph. 6:20). It is only a brief parenthesis; he did not dwell on his hardships. But the pathos in this passing remark is as profound as it is real, and this stands out clearly in the last words of his speech at Caesarea: 'I would to God, that whether with little or with much, not thou only, but also all that hear me this day, might become such as I am, *except these bonds*' (Acts 26:29). But in spite of his bonds, his great desire was that he might have grace to make that great mystery *manifest* to all. He used the same word which he had chosen when he declared that he carried about in his body the dying of the Lord Jesus that the life of the Lord Jesus might be *manifest* in his body (2 Cor. 4:10-11). The full proclamation of Christ to the Gentiles was for him a solemn obligation; necessity was laid upon his heart (1 Cor. 9:16). He had no choice; he sought to speak as he knew that he *ought to speak*. Such an open door for preaching, and such grace to preach with boldness, were in fact made good to him while he was in Rome: he dwelt in his own house and taught the truth about the Lord Jesus to all who came to him (Acts 28:30-31).

The text reverts from the particular situation in which he found himself and goes on to a fresh exhortation of a practical character: 'Walk in wisdom toward them that are without, redeeming the time' (4:5). There is a close correspondence in thought between this text and the Petrine exhortation about right conduct toward the Gentiles: 'that, wherein they speak against you as evil-doers, they may by your good works which they behold, glorify God in the day of visitation' (1 Pet. 2:12). Paul knew that there were some who had brought the doctrine of grace into disrepute because of the argument that it was right to sin so that grace might abound; and that there were others who had crude and distorted conceptions of their way of life and worship as a result of rumours current in pagan society. It was therefore of the utmost concern for the honour of Christ that they should give the lie to such slander by their manner of life. They were so to *walk* that men could make no mistake. This became a favourite injunction in his Letters (cf. Eph. 4:1; 1 Thess. 2:12). He had in fact urged this duty on his readers in the same terms in an earlier paragraph: they were 'to walk worthily of the Lord unto all well-pleasing' (1:10). It was strengthened in this verse by the call to walk *in wisdom*: they were to use the sound common sense of sober judgment in order to commend the truth to *them that are without*. This phrase makes it clear that those whom he had in view were the Gentiles who were strangers to the household of faith. An element of urgency lends point to the last clause: *redeeming the time*. This phrase in the Ephesian Epistle had an eye to days of persecution: they were to buy up the passing moments because the days were evil (Eph. 5:16). But its special application in this verse was to their pagan neighbours: they were never to let the chance slip for walking in such a way as would commend the cause of Christ.

The next words go on to show how eager Paul was that his converts should share in the grace and wisdom of speech which he had asked them to pray for on his behalf: 'Let your speech be always with grace, seasoned with salt' (4:6). This verse may be compared with a similar injunction in the Epistle to the Ephesians: 'Let no corrupt speech proceed out of your mouth, but such as is good for edifying as the need may be, that it may give grace to them that hear' (Eph. 4:29). The word *speech* stands for all forms of language in talking or discourse, but it especially refers in this context to conversation with non-Christians. The Lord Himself had once voiced the solemn warning: 'Every idle word that men shall speak, they shall give account thereof in the day of judgment' (Matt. 12:36). Conversation helps to manifest character; character helps to determine destiny. Therefore our speech should be *always with grace*. The word *always* has the quality of an absolute: there is never a time when our conversation should not be marked by grace. This is amplified by the direction that it should be *seasoned with salt*, and this remark may be linked with the Lord's command: 'Have salt in yourselves, and be at peace one with another' (Mark 9:50). Salt is something that penetrates; its influence is pervasive; its action is hidden and unseen; its effects are to provide taste and preserve from corruption. This is why salt is to season our speech, to give it a pleasant savour, to make it the reverse of an insipid utterance. But the Ephesian injunction shows that it will also preserve conversation from all that is bad and corrupt, and will make it sweet and wholesome. Therefore all speech should be *seasoned with salt* as the grace that makes all conversation pure and pleasant to the taste of mind and spirit.

Such a rule for speech and conversation had an apologetic aim: 'that ye may know how ye ought to answer each one' (4:6). Sins of speech have always been the cause of strife and scandal; grace alone can banish all such unseemly elements. Therefore they were to make sure that their speech was so rich in grace that it would be free from all offence, and that they would know how to meet the cavils and questions of those who were 'without' (4:5). It was imperative that they should not avoid pagan inquiry, nor yet seek to evade candid objection, and they would need divine guidance if they were to speak the right word in all circumstances (cf. Luke 21:14-15). Therefore by the grace of God they were to observe this sound rule of conversation so as to know how to talk with non-Christian neighbours (Cf. Matt. 10:19). This is brought out still more clearly in the Petrine exhortation: 'Being ready always to give answer to every man that asketh you a reason concerning the hope that is in you, yet with meekness and fear' (1 Pet. 3:15). To be ready to make answer to all who ask for a reason is thus wisely coupled with the spirit of gentleness and reverence. They were to meet questions, not with skilfully adapted argument, but with lovingly persuasive courtesy; they were to have recourse to the honest good sense that will state the truth with candour and will seek to conciliate all who are still without. This called for an intelligent respect for the character or the attitude of the person who asked, and it would not refuse to give a clear account of the reason why Christ in them was 'the hope of glory' (1:27). Those who are in Christ must freely avow just what this means, and the basic factor is one of great simplicity: I am what I am because He is what He is (1 Cor. 15:10). Therefore all our conversation should be relevant to the company in which we find ourselves, if by any means we are to win some (1 Cor. 9:19–22).

We are all like those men who had need to remind themselves that they would stand or fall before 'a Master in heaven' (4:1): our prayers, our walk, and our conversation must be hallowed by the constant recollection of His presence. History can not tabulate how far the spread of the Gospel has been due to such rules as these; we may single out in particular the power of good conversation. Missionary annals have always been able to point to the gossip of the bazaars as one of the ways in which the Name of Christ has travelled abroad. Thomas Becon in the morning of the English Reformation was one of the younger men in Cambridge who used to meet in the White Horse Inn for godly conversation. 'So oft as I was in their company', he wrote, 'methought I was . . . quietly placed in the new glorious Jerusalem'.[1] John Bunyan has described how he found three or four women in one of the streets of Bedford: they sat at a door in the sun and spoke about the new birth as the work of God in their own hearts. It was joy that made them speak, and there was such grace in what they said that it seemed to Bunyan 'as if they had found a new world . . . and were not to be reckoned among their neighbours'.[2] Charles Simeon established his conversation parties in his rooms at King's College, Cambridge, in 1812 so that he might engage undergraduates in the informal dialogue of young men at a tea party. They were schools of manly thought and common sense in dealing with the problems which spring from the greatest issues in life. Martyn and Thomason, Sargent and Sowerby, and a host of others, never knew more of the communion of saints on earth than in his rooms at such meetings.[3] So then, in the widest sense of the word, let our *conversation* ever be such as becomes the Gospel of Christ (cf. Phil. 1:27).

[1] Thomas Becon: The Catechism with other Pieces (Parker Society) p. 426.
[2] John Bunyan: *Grace Abounding to the Chief of Sinners*; cf. *The Works of John Bunyan* (Offor edition) Vol. 1 p. 10.
[3] William Carus: *Memoirs of The Life of The Rev. Charles Simeon*, 1847, p. 271.

Chapter Twenty-four

A Brother Beloved

'No longer as a servant, but more than a servant, a
brother beloved, specially to me, but how much rather
to thee, both in the flesh and in the Lord'.

THE EPISTLE TO PHILEMON

THE EPISTLE to Philemon is the third in a group of short prison
Letters, and some points of comparison stand out clearly. The
Epistle to the Ephesians was in all probability an apostolic
encyclical to the churches throughout Proconsular Asia; the
Epistle to the Colossians was a special letter for one particular
congregation in the Valley of the Lycus; the Epistle to Philemon
was an appeal to a single convert on a semi-private issue. There
were many close links between the three Letters in a variety of
detail and circumstance. The Epistle to the Ephesians refers to
the fact that Paul was 'the prisoner of Christ Jesus' (3:1), subject
to 'tribulations' on behalf of his Gentile converts (3:13), 'the
prisoner of the Lord' (4:1), 'an ambassador in chains' (6:20). The
Epistle to the Colossians refers to the fact that he could rejoice in
his 'sufferings' (1:24), and this meant that he was 'in bonds' (4:3,
18). The Epistle to Philemon refers to the fact that he was 'a
prisoner of Christ Jesus' (1, 9), and that he was 'in bonds' (10).
The marked correspondence of this language in each Letter is all
the more interesting in view of the number of names which are
common to them. Timothy is twice linked with Paul in the
salutation (Col. 1:1; Philemon 1). Tychicus was twice described
as 'the beloved brother and faithful minister in the Lord' (Eph.
6:21-22; Col. 4:7-8). Epaphras was mentioned as 'our beloved
fellow servant' (Col. 1:7) and a 'fellow prisoner in Christ Jesus'
(Philemon 23). Onesimus and Archippus, Mark and Aristar-

chus, Luke and Demas, all find mention in Colossians and Philemon. There are only four names which are mentioned only once and in one Letter: Jesus Justus (Col. 4:11); Nymphas (Col. 4:15); Philemon and Apphia (Philemon 1, 2). Such facts make it impossible not to recognise how closely these three Letters are related to each other in time and circumstance.

Thus it may be assumed that Paul employed Tychicus as the scribe and bearer of these Epistles, and that Onesimus accompanied him when he set out for Roman Asia and the Valley of the Lycus. The Epistle to Philemon is the only surviving example of the private correspondence which must have passed between Paul and his converts. It affords a unique picture of his personal relations with those who were his sons in the Gospel. His great object in this Letter was transparent, but delicate: it was to reconcile a runaway slave with his master. Onesimus had betrayed his master's trust, stolen from his household, and become a fugitive in fear of his life. He tried to lose himself in Rome, the great city cess-pool for the dregs of humanity, but was soon in danger of being overwhelmed by loneliness and need. Perhaps it was a chance meeting with Epaphras who also came from Colossae which proved the turning point in his experience. Epaphras introduced him to Paul in prison, and Paul led him to put his trust in Christ. The fugitive from Colossae found himself under the divine arrest; the slave was a free man in Christ. Paul soon came to love him as a son in the faith and to find in him a source of daily comfort in his imprisonment. But the imperious necessity to do all that was right compelled him to send the slave back to his master, and he wrote this Letter in order to provide a bridge between the one and the other. The master and servant relationship was not denied; it was caught up in a new and richer relationship in which master and slave were seen to have become brethren in Christ. It is for this reason that this Letter is so remarkable as an illustration of the social impact of the Gospel. Here was proof, if proof were required, that in God's sight, there is neither bond nor free since Christ is all, and in all (Col. 3:11).

The Epistle to Philemon invites comparison with a Letter which Pliny the Younger wrote to Sabinianus in order to plead the cause of a certain freedman.[1] Pliny's appeal was made on the grounds of humanity, and in diction and style, it was preoccupied with his reputation. 'Your freedman', he wrote, 'with whom you said you were angry, has come to me, and, flinging himself at my feet, clung to me as though I were you. He wept a great deal, asked me many things, and left much unsaid; in short, he convinced me that he was genuinely sorry. I believe he has mended his ways, because he realises he did wrong. You are angry, I know, and that you have reason to be, I also know. But mercy is most praiseworthy when there is a most just reason for anger. You loved the man in the past and, I trust, will love him again; meanwhile it is sufficient if you allow yourself to be prevailed upon. You may always be angry with him again if he deserves it, and you will have more excuse for this after once being successfully entreated. Make some concession to his youth, to his tears, and to you own kindness. Don't torment him, or for that matter, yourself; for you will torment yourself, when it is you, so mild-tempered a man, who is angry. I am afraid to appear to be using compulsion, and not entreaty, if I add my prayers to his; yet I will do this, and as fully and copiously as I have pointedly and severely scolded the fellow, warning him firmly that I will never again make the request. This I said to him, for he needed the fright, but it was not meant for you; for perhaps I shall ask you again, and the second time, obtain what I ask, provided that it is only what is fit for me to ask and you to grant'.

This may be seen as a backdrop for the study of the Epistle to Philemon which excels in charm, in tact, in humanity and delicacy, in the pathos of its appeal on the ground of Christian fellowship: 'Paul, a prisoner of Christ Jesus, and Timothy our brother, to Philemon our beloved and fellow worker, and to Apphia our sister, and to Archippus our fellow soldier, and to the church in thy house: grace to you and peace from God our Father and the Lord Jesus Christ' (1, 2, 3). Paul had dropped his designation as an apostle with its implicit note of authority, and used instead a phrase which would prepare the way for an entreaty

[1] Pliny, *Letters* 9.21 (Translation by Miss Cynthia Begbie of the Latin Department in the University of Sydney).

on the ground of compassion. Timothy's name was linked with his own in view of their intimate connection with each other while in Ephesus. The Letter was addressed in their joint-names to an ordinary household in the Phrygian town of Colossae, and the natural inference is that Philemon and Apphia and Archippus were all members of one family. Philemon had been converted through Paul's ministry while Paul was in Ephesus (19), and like Nymphas in the sister town of Laodicea, had made his house a home for the church in Colossae (Col. 4:15). It seems safe to assume that Apphia was Philemon's wife, and it is probable that Archippus was their son. This small household of faith in the heart of a strong pagan community affords its own valuable insight into the now rapidly expanding radius of the Gospel. In the Epistle to the Colossians, there was a short message for Archippus with a salutary exhortation: 'Take heed to the ministry which thou hast received in the Lord, that thou fulfil it' (Col. 4:17). But it was to all three that Paul addressed himself with his customary salutation of grace and peace in the Name of *God our Father and the Lord Jesus Christ.* [2]

As in all the Pauline Letters, with the exception of the Epistle to the Galatians, the salutation is followed by thanksgiving and remembrance in prayer: 'I thank my God always, making mention of thee in my prayers, hearing of thy love and of the faith which thou hast toward the Lord Jesus and toward all the saints' (4, 5). Apphia and Archippus drop out of sight, as the use of the second person singular shows (cf. *thy house*); Philemon as head of that household was the person to whom Paul would appeal. He had made use of this identical phrase, *I thank my God*, in three other Epistles (Rom. 1:8; 1 Cor. 1:4; Phil. 1:3). Such words provide one of the more striking glimpses into his own heart both as a servant of God and as a guide to His people. He was deeply conscious of the need to care for particular converts as well as for 'all the churches' (2 Cor. 11:28), and he remembered Philemon when he lifted his heart to God with a truly thankful sense of all God's goodness to him. It was probably Epaphras who had spoken

---

[2] cf. Rom. 1:7; 1 Cor. 1:3; 2 Cor. 1:2; Gal. 1:3; Eph. 1:2; Phil. 1:2; Col. 1:2; 1 Thess. 1:2; 2 Thess. 1:2.

to him about the love and faith which marked Philemon's character, but there is a curious element in the manner in which it
was expressed. J. B. Lightfoot held that Paul had violated the
strict order of thought and had turned the last part of the sentence
round so as to produce an example of the figure of speech known
as chiasm (cf. Gal. 4:4–5).[3] He had uttered his thoughts aloud in
the sequence in which they had come to his mind and had not
paid any special regard to their logical arrangement. Thus the
references to love and faith should be distributed cross-wise to *all
the saints* and to *the Lord Jesus* respectively (cf. Col. 1:3–4). The
real meaning of the verse as a whole is that Paul had heard of the
faith which Philemon exercised *toward the Lord Jesus* and of the
love which he showed *toward all the saints*.

The evidence of Philemon's love for the saints was seen in the
fact that the church met in his house, and this thought is pursued
in the next words: 'That the fellowship of thy faith may become
effectual, in the knowledge of every good thing which is in you,
unto Christ. For I had much joy and comfort in thy love, because
the hearts of the saints have been refreshed through thee, brother'
(6, 7). The expression of thanksgiving thus passed at once into
prayer that all the good in which he rejoiced might grow. The
word *fellowship* is used here in the sense of a charitable sharing of
his substance with the poorer members of that little congregation
(cf. Rom. 15:26; 2 Cor. 9:13). Therefore his prayer was that
Philemon's generous conduct would make for the constant
increase of true knowledge (cf. Eph. 4:13; Col. 1:9). It was
Philemon's benefit in this respect rather than the effect of his life
on others of which Paul was thinking: he would grow in understanding of 'all the good that is ours in Christ' (R.S.V.). This most
comprehensive vision points to the fact that the glory of Christ is
'the true aim of the true life of grace'.[4] Paul went on to disclose
the real motive for his initial words of thanksgiving. It sprang
from the joy and encouragement which had cheered and
strengthened his heart when the news of Philemon's generous

[3] J. B. Lightfoot: *The Epistles of St Paul: Colossians and Philemon* p. 334.
[4] H. C. G. Moule: *The Epistles to the Colossians and to Philemon* (Camb. Bible for
Schools and Colleges) p. 170.

conduct reached him in his prison quarters. He was himself refreshed when he heard how *the hearts of the saints* had been refreshed (cf. 20; 2 Cor. 7:13). The last word in the Greek text of this verse was the warm and kindly term of address, *brother*, and the emphatic position of this word of Christian affection helps to convey a most winning sense of friendship (cf. Gal. 6:18). Paul placed himself on the level of true equality with Philemon in terms that would provide a most skilful preparation for the appeal he was about to make.

There was infinite wistfulness in the spirit in which he went on to lay bare all that was in his heart: 'Wherefore, though I have all boldness in Christ to enjoin thee that which is befitting, yet for love's sake I rather beseech, being such a one as Paul the aged, and now a prisoner also of Christ Jesus' (8, 9). Paul knew that he might have spoken with the full weight of his apostolic authority: 'I am bold enough in Christ to command you to do what is required' (R.S.V.). He could say this in view of his office *in Christ*, and fellowship with Philemon in Him would have made such outspokenness acceptable. But he chose to entreat rather than to command, and the ground on which he did so was *for love's sake*. This may have meant the bond of strong personal affection between the apostle and Philemon. At all events, he went on to press home his appeal by speaking of himself as *such a one as Paul the aged*. It is arguable whether this meant *because* he was such or *although* he was such. H. C. G. Moule argued that the former fits the context better, for the clause would then mean that he spoke in this way in order to strengthen his entreaty for compassion. He who had the right to command chose to appeal on the ground that he was now fast ageing. This would touch the chord of human pathos, and its effect would be enhanced by the reference to his circumstances as *a prisoner of Christ Jesus*. [5] But the phrase *Paul the aged* may be rendered *Paul an ambassador* (cf. R.V.M; R.S.V.); the two words are almost identical in Greek. J. B. Lightfoot argued that this meant that he chose to plead this cause on the basis of love *although* he could have urged it as one who was

---

[5] H. C. G. Moule. *ibid*. p. 172.

'an ambassador in bonds' (cf. Eph. 6:20).[6] But the dominant emphasis in each case falls on the phrase *for love's sake*.

Paul then reminded Philemon that he himself was now a man in bonds before he went on to name the bondman for whom he meant to plead: 'I beseech thee for my child, whom I have begotten in my bonds, Onesimus, who was aforetime unprofitable to thee, but now is profitable to thee and to me' (10, 11). The word *beseech* is caught up and carried on from the verse before, and the entreaty itself becomes explicit. It was a most tender appeal for one whom he described as *my son* (A.V.) or *my child* (R.V.). He saw himself as the father-in-God to this runaway delinquent because he had *begotten* him while in prison. He used the same figure of speech elsewhere: 'In Christ Jesus, I begat you through the Gospel' (1 Cor. 4:15). But this was more than a figure of speech; it would express the most intimate affection on the part of Paul for Onesimus. If more pathos could add yet more effect, it was conveyed in the idea that he was the child of his own captivity, born while he was in bonds. He had held back the name thus far, but now at last it was disclosed. The word *Onesimus*, like the word *brother* just a few verses before, stands last in the Greek text of this sentence; it was allowed to wait until the ground had been fully prepared. Onesimus was a common slave-name because it meant *profitable*, and a verse in parenthesis took up this thought with an affectionate piece of word-play. Onesimus had been untrue to his own name; he had proved an 'unprofitable servant' (cf. Luke 17:10). But this brief and delicate allusion to his delinquency went far enough, for now, as a result of his new birth through the Gospel, he had become truly *profitable*. Philemon would find this as true in Colossae as Paul had done in Rome: he would prove as useful to *thee* as he had done to *me*. It was a telling and skilful testimony which could hardly be brushed aside.

The next words make it clear that this Letter was to accompany Onesimus as he made the long hard journey back to Philemon's home in Colossae: 'Whom I have sent back to thee in his own person, that is, my very heart: whom I would fain have kept with me, that in thy behalf he might minister unto me in the bonds of

---

[6] J. B. Lightfoot, *ibid*. pp. 335-337.

the Gospel: but without thy mind I would do nothing; that thy goodness should not be as of necessity, but of free will' (12, 13, 14). Paul here made use of the epistolary aorist for the present tense of the verb: *I sent* (cf. Col. 4:8). He was about to send him back and this purpose was so firm that he spoke as though he had in fact done so. It is impossible to say how much faith and self-denial are packed into this phrase: it is only hinted at in the short parenthesis which says that it was as though he were to send his own heart. He more than half wished that he could keep him at his own side; he was only stopped from doing so by other weighty reasons. It was as though Onesimus might have cared for him on behalf of his master, and that was a gentle hint that Philemon's devotion could always be relied upon. Then he referred once more to his imprisonment: such *bonds* were an oblique appeal to affection and compassion. But he declared that he would do nothing without Philemon's approval because he was anxious for his *goodness* to shine in true beauty. He would not let that goodness wear the mildest look of constraint, and the phrase *as it were* (A.V.) softened the comment on *necessity*. He was sending Onesimus back because to detain him would have been to take advantage of Philemon's goodness, whether he were willing or not; and that goodness was such that it ought to flow from his own free will.

Paul had another argument which was meant to impress Philemon with a sense of divine providence in all that had happened: 'For perhaps he was therefore parted from thee for a season, that thou shouldest have him for ever; no longer as a servant, but more than a servant, a brother beloved, specially to me, but how much rather to thee, both in the flesh and in the Lord' (15, 16). Paul's quiet tact was sustained as he tried to interpret the misconduct of Onesimus in a new light. It was not so much that he had fled from bondage; he was *parted* from his master. Joseph had excused his brethren in the same way: 'God did send me before you' (Gen. 45:5). This absence was only *for a season* (cf. 2 Cor. 7:8; Gal. 2:5); he would return once and for all. The phrase *for ever* takes in all time and looks on to eternity; it spoke of the absolute permanence of his restoration. The next words fill this out with a moving simplicity. Onesimus might still belong to the slave class, but he could no longer be thought of as if he were no more than a slave. Paul did not speak of manumission, but he made it plain that the change which had been wrought in him was real, whether or not Philemon was willing to recognise the fact. He was *more than a slave*; he was now a *beloved brother* (R.S.V.). Such words were as bold a statement as the society of Greece or Rome had yet heard on such class issues, for it meant that Onesimus had been made free and was of kin with all the saints in Christ.[7] This was true *most of all* in Paul's own case; Onesimus was as dear to him as a son. But to convey his argument to Philemon, he strained all the rules of grammar and said that he was *more than most of all* dear to Philemon as a brother.[8] This was now in fact a spiritual reality, 'both in the flesh and in the Lord'.

Paul pressed home this appeal on the basis of his own fellowship with Philemon: 'If then thou countest me a partner, receive him as myself. But if he hath wronged thee at all, or oweth thee aught, put that to mine account; I Paul write it with mine own hand, I will repay it: that I say not unto thee how that thou owest to me even thine own self besides' (17, 18, 19). Paul now ventured to say that if Philemon considered him to be his friend and fellow, he would welcome Onesimus as though it were himself. He piled affectionate terms on Onesimus: he was his *child* (10), his *very heart* (12), his other *self* (17). Nor could he let matters rest at that point. He went on to state a hypothesis which may well have described the truth. Onesimus had been guilty of some offence; he had wronged his master before he had made his escape. Therefore if he stood in his debt, that was to be put down to Paul's account. This was confirmed by the introduction of his own name in the formal spirit of a personal signature: *I Paul write it with mine own hand* (cf. Col. 4:18). The whole undertaking is summed up in a phrase of two words, one of which was in Greek an emphatic personal pronoun: *I will repay it*. This was *to say*

---

[7] H. C. G. Moule, *ibid*. p. 175.

[8] J. B. Lightfoot, *ibid*. p. 341. Compare the phrase 'less than the least' (Eph. 3:8).

nothing (R.S.V.) of the fact that Philemon was so much more indebted to him. J. B. Lightfoot points out that there is 'a suppressed thought' in this clause (cf. 2 Cor. 9:4), [9] Onesimus would be restored to his master as a new man; such a fact would cover any loss which had been incurred at the time when he ran away. [10] Thus Philemon was indebted to him even in this respect, and this took no account of what he owed *besides*. That was something which could not be assessed in worth; it was no less than *thine own self*.

The whole appeal moved on to a climax with a final affectionate request: 'Yea, brother, let me have joy of thee in the Lord: refresh my heart in Christ. Having confidence in thine obedience, I write unto thee, knowing that thou wilt do even beyond what I say. But withal prepare me also a lodging: for I hope that through your prayers, I shall be granted unto you' (20, 21, 22). The *yea* lends force to what he had to say (cf. Phil. 4:3), and the address to him as his *brother* strengthens the tenderness and earnestness of his appeal. Then the emphatic personal pronoun served to identify the cause of Onesimus with his own: May I find joy in thee! [11] He had put forth all his strength in pleading on behalf of Onesimus; now he argued that this was in effect like pleading for himself. *To give him joy in the Lord* would be to *refresh* his heart *in Christ*, and Philemon was already well known as one who had often refreshed the hearts of God's people (cf. 7). Paul felt so sure that he would respond to this appeal that he wrote with the calm knowledge that he would do more than was asked. Did he think in terms of manumission? Was he hoping that Philemon would emancipate his servant? He did not say; but if this were the thought behind his words, their quiet restraint was all the more remarkable. He did not press his suit further, but went on to ask that a room should be prepared for him. He made no prophecy where none was authorised, [12] but he intimated that it was his intention to travel to Colossae when his release took place. There was more

[9] J. B. Lightfoot, *ibid.* p. 344.
[10] H. C. G. Moule, *ibid.* p. 176.
[11] J. B. Lightfoot, *ibid.* p. 344.
[12] H. C. G. Moule, *ibid.* p. 177.

than general interest in this remark; it would add a new and compelling tenderness to his appeal. He would come to see for himself that his hopes for Onesimus were not disappointed. And more; he would hope to discover that his confidence in Philemon was justified.

The whole Letter came to a close with the customary greetings of those who were with him at the time of writing: 'Epaphras, my fellow prisoner in Christ Jesus, saluteth thee; and so do Mark, Aristarchus, Demas, Luke, my fellow workers. The grace of our Lord Jesus Christ be with your spirit. Amen' (23, 24, 25). Epaphras was a resident in the town of Colossae (Col. 4:12), and had been its evangelist (Col. 1:7). He had come to visit Paul in prison with news of the churches in the Valley of the Lycus, and he was so often with him in his quarters that he could be described as his fellow captive. Mark and Aristarchus belonged to 'the circumcision' (Col. 4:10-11); Luke and Demas were both Gentiles. They may all have been of Greek or Asiatic origin and would be well-known to Philemon by name if not in person.[13] Perhaps the most interesting name in this group from the viewpoint of this Letter was that of Mark, for his early experience as one of Paul's fellow workers had been marked by total failure. But he had been restored, and Paul was to declare that Mark was *profitable* to him in his ministry (2 Tim. 4:11). It was the same word that he had used about Onesimus in this Letter (cf. 11). Luke and Aristarchus were both tried and steadfast friends and fellow workers; Demas alone out of this group was to forsake him for love of the world (2 Tim. 4:10). The brief salutation in the name of these friends then gave way to words of farewell which were identical with the form of farewell in the Epistle to the Galatians (Gal. 6:24). It was the prayer that the grace of God, seen in the saving presence of Christ, would be with their spirit: and he referred to *your spirit*, the spirit of you all, as if the whole household of Philemon, and Apphia, and Archippus, were animated by one single spirit in Christ Jesus.[14]

Onesimus the slave is thus described as a *brother beloved* (16);

[13] J. B. Lightfoot, *ibid*. p. 344.
[14] H. C. G. Moule, *ibid*. p. 178.

and slaves such as Onesimus who had found the secret of life in Christ Jesus were to hold believing masters like Philemon in true respect 'because they are brethren' (1 Tim. 6:2). Such words were in 'fatal antithesis' to the principle, if not to the existence, of the whole slave system.[15] This was nobly demonstrated in the persecution which broke out at Lyons and Vienne in A.D. 177. Pothinus, an old man of ninety, was the first who had to appear, since he was the bishop. He was pelted by the mob and died in prison. Another Christian who had been seized was the slave-girl Blandina; it was thought that she would quickly succumb to the authorities. But she was to wear out those who were sent to conduct her torture and at last they had to admit that they could not break her spirit. The grim record of the appalling cruelties which she endured as day followed day makes up an almost incredible story. She was impaled on a stake so that wild beasts could tear her down; but they refused to touch her, and she was taken back to prison. She was scourged; she was mauled and dragged about by beasts; she was roasted in an iron chair; she was put in a net and tossed by a wild bull. Her body was so scarred and broken that the wonder was how she had survived at all. But the end came at last. Paul himself had never offered a more glorious defiance to the might of this world than she did on that day. She was driven, naked, into the arena before the eyes of a vast crowd, but she faced the gladiator's final sword-thrust with a smiling welcome as she lifted up her eyes to heaven.[16] Philemon and Onesimus, Blandina and Pothinus, Perpetua and Felicitas, were to teach the world that Christ has made bond and free altogether equal, for Christ in them was the hope of glory (Col. 1:27).

---

[15] H. C. G. Moule, *ibid.* p. 175.
[16] H. M. Gwatkin: *Early Church History to A.D. 313.* Vol. I pp. 157–163; 234.